F

LUCIA CAPACCHIONE, PH. D.

Recovery of Your Inner Child

A FIRESIDE BOOK

Published by Simon & Schuster

F

SIMON & SCHUSTER / FIRESIDE

Rockefeller Center
1230 Avenue of the Americas
New York, New York 10020

FIRESIDE and colophon are registered trademarks
of Simon & Schuster

DESIGNED BY BLACK ANGUS DESIGN GROUP
Manufactured in the United States of America

28 29 30

Library of Congress Cataloging in Publication Data

Capacchione, Lucia, Ph. D.
    Recovery of your inner child / Lucia Capacchione.
        p. cm.
    "A Fireside book."
    1. Inner child. 2. Self-actualization (Psychology) 3. Writing—
Psychological aspects. 4. Drawing, Psychology of. 5. Left- and
right-handedness. 6. Cerebral dominance. I. Title.
    BF698.35.I55C36   1991
    158'.1—dc20   90-46317
                                                   CIP

ISBN 0-671-74026-1
0-671-70135-5 (Pbk.)

Grateful acknowledgement is made to Newcastle Publishing Co., Inc. for per-
mission to reprint the drawings on pages 28, 29, and 30 from *The Power of Your
Other Hand*, by Lucia Capacchione.
Copyright © 1988 by Lucia Capacchione.

The author is also grateful to Sydna Bell-Windeyer for the use of her drawings on
pages 191–193, 198, 199, 220–222, and 250, from an unpublished manuscript.

To my creative associates
Jim Strohecker and Nancy Shaw Strohecker
for their invaluable expertise, contribution, and support
through all phases of this project.
Without their collaboration
this book would not have been possible.
Special thanks to Jim Strohecker for his
role in the conceptual development of this book
particularly regarding his insights into
the Triune Brain Theory and
the research of Dr. Álvaro López-Watermann.

Heartfelt thanks to all those who have participated
in my Inner Child workshops over the years
especially those who attended the Embracing Your Inner Child
Workshop at La Casa de Maria
as I was completing the manuscript of this book.
Without your stories, drawings, dialogues, and loving support
this book would not have been possible.

CONTRIBUTORS:

Betty Anderson
Geraldine Berns
Kathy Bevacqua
Anne Boundy
Judy Bradley
Ron Brookshire
Molly Campbell
Penelope Cariffe
Faith Ann Cavalier
Anne Leigh Courtney
Kay Cox
Bette Davis
Joan Delzangle
Delores Estrada
Michele Feher
Rainie Fross
Susan Gant
Don Gay
Bonne Goltzreiser
Susan Gonzalez
Tracey Hansen
Nancy Kane

Archie Lawrence
Elizabeth Lord
Rosa Manriquez
Sue Maxwell
Dee Nicholson
Carol Parrish
Kathy Price
Tom Reilly
Maria Rodriguez
Beverly Sibley
Katherine Smith
Jim Strohecker
Nancy Shaw Strohecker
Lola Taylor
Janel Temple
Tricia Thompson
Kate Tieman
Geri Towle
Manda Washburn
Christina Wilson
Lori Zann

Dedicated, with love, to Sri Bhagawan Nityananda, a great Indian saint and master teacher of the Siddha lineage, whose company was sought by sages and children alike.

And to my daughters Celia and Aleta, and my grandchildren, for teaching me the way of the Child.

Author's Note

Table of Contents

CONTENTS

Introduction

I recommend this book to any adult child of a dysfunctional family who wants to strengthen or go deeper into the process of healing their Child Within.

Experiential recovery aids are an important part of recovery, and here Lucia Capacchione provides numerous guidelines, exercises, and pearls of wisdom to help you access, know, and be your true self—your Child Within.

Alice Miller, a pioneer in the recovery field, said, "Only when I make room for the voice of the child within me do I feel myself to be genuine and creative."[1] We have heard empowering messages such as these throughout history but didn't know how to use them until now. The Old Testament prophets told us, "The wolf also shall dwell with the lamb, and the leopard shall lie down with the kid, and the calf and the young lion and the fatling together, and a little child shall lead them." (Isaiah 11:6). And Christ said it more clearly, "Unless you change and become like little children, you will not enter the Kingdom of Heaven." (Matthew 11:25, 18:3; Luke 18:16-17).

[1] A. Miller, *The Drama of the Gifted Child.* (New York: Harper & Row, 1983).

The kingdom is what we in the recovery movement call "serenity," and what *A Course in Miracles*[2] describes as God's Will for us: complete peace and joy. To become like a little child is to realize and live from our True Selves, the Child Within. And, there is a second meaning here: that we are each a child of God and are thus dependent on our Higher Power in a healthy way, as the *Course* describes. In this sense we are co-creators of our lives.

But growing up in a troubled, unhealthy, or dysfunctional family may have been very painful. So to survive, the True Self went into hiding deep within the unconscious part of itself. The Child went into hiding. To survive, we relied on the false or co-dependent self to take over and run our lives, even though it didn't know how. We got so used to this false self that we now have a hard time letting it go and reclaiming our True Selves.

The absence of the Child Within leaves a painful feeling of emptiness, like something is missing in our lives. Have you ever felt that? Relying on the false self, we try to fill our emptiness with all kinds of people, places, things, behaviors, and experiences from outside of ourselves. It can take us a long time to realize that doing so doesn't work; it doesn't work because the absence of things from the outside didn't cause the emptiness. What caused it was that the Child within us went into hiding. As a result, we lost our True Selves and thereby our ability to connect with others and with God in a meaningful way.

The only way to fill our emptiness is to realize the True Self within us and experientially connect it to God. When we do that and complete our unfinished business, we are healed. Then we are free to co-create a successful and enjoyable life for ourselves. Only recently have we known how to co-create our healing in this way. I have described it, as have others, and in this book Lucia Capacchione does so also, with an emphasis on the experiential methods of reading, reacting, writing, drawing, reacting some more, and sharing.

In recovery, a way we can begin to experience our powerful inner life more and more is to choose one or more experiential techniques that provide a safe and focused method for actually using our Real or True Selves. This book does just that. It provides a structure so that we can focus on being Real, and its messages and guidance are safe. It comes from one of the great teachers and therapists of our day.

Charles L. Whitfield, M.D.,
Baltimore, MD, October 1990

[2] *A Course in Miracles.* (Tiburon, CA: Foundation for Inner Peace, 1976).

Finding My Inner Child

Turning fifty was a milestone for me, a time to stop and look in the rear-view mirror at five decades of global change. In that mirror I see three major wars, a cure for polio, the birth of television and computers, the rise and fall of dictators, the assassination of a U.S. president, man on the moon, and the creation and collapse of the Berlin Wall.

I first see myself as a beaming, apple-cheeked toddler sitting on my grandmother's lap, then as an excited youngster visiting the sound stages of MGM Studios with my film editor father, and as a uniformed schoolgirl enduring the rules and authority figures in parochial schools. Later, I see myself as a teenager living for Saturday art classes, where my talents were nurtured by an inspiring teacher and artist.

Each decade after that seemed to have its own personal theme and flavor. The fifties were a time for completing college and a degree in art. For me the sixties were about marriage, family, and artistic achievement. On the larger level they were also about human rights, and I helped fight Johnson's War on Poverty as a Head Start director. By the decade's end, the Women's Movement was fully launched. Like many of my sisters, I was juggling a number of roles, i.e., wife, mother, artist, and educator.

Then, one day, the bottom dropped out as the seventies began. It was to become a decade of personal crises: the break-up of my marriage and business partnership, the end of my parents' marriage, confrontation with a life-threatening disease, and a radical career and lifestyle change. When my ten-year marriage ended abruptly in January of 1970, I was totally unprepared. My fast-paced life had left precious little time for listening to the Vulnerable Child within my own heart. Success had pulled me outward. A public life is hard on the Inner Child—the feeling part of us that needs nurturing, that loves to play and explore, that loves naps, and that thrives on simply "being" instead of achieving. Within three years of my divorce, the pressures of professional work and single parenting threw me into a severe health crisis: a life-threatening disease affecting the collagen, or connective tissue in the body.

After a long series of mishaps at the medical clinic where I was receiving treatment, I went in search of an alternative approach to healing. Without realizing it, I had the most powerful healing tool right under my own nose. While writing and drawing in a personal journal that I had started keeping at the beginning of the illness, I realized that journaling my feelings was actually helping me feel better—physically and emotionally. That discovery was destined eventually to lead me into a new career as an art therapist and author. However, at the time I began keeping a journal, I was simply struggling for my own survival.

The insights I gained from this profoundly personal form of writing and drawing prompted me to seek therapy. It was in therapy that I first became conscious of my Inner Child: the vulnerable, feeling, spontaneous, creative self that was crying out to be heard. Imprisoned in my grown-up persona, she wanted out. The only way she could attract my attention was through an illness that forced me to go inside and listen to her needs. Through Gestalt role-playing in therapy and journal writing and drawing done with both hands, I came to know this very real Child who lives within me. She lives in my body, in my feelings and intuition, and she has brought me understanding and a new life.

It is the spirit of this Inner Child who speaks to you throughout the pages of this book. It is this same spirit who wants you to find and honor your own true Self, to become your own loving parent, and to heal every area of your life. For the Inner Child holds the key to intimacy in relationships, physical energy, and well-being, as well as enthusiasm and creativity in work. An active and healthy Inner Child is one of the best preventions for burn-out and disease. It is the source of humor, play, and rejuvenation—the spice of life. When the Inner Child is allowed to be itself and dwell in your heart, it can lead you to a wellspring of infinite wisdom and joy.

LUCIA CAPACCHIONE, Ph.D., ATR
Santa Monica, California
April 1990.

PART I

Discovering Your Inner Child

The Inner Child is a powerful presence. It dwells at the core of our being. Imagine a healthy, happy toddler. As you picture this child in your mind's eye, sense its aliveness. With great enthusiasm it constantly explores the environment. It knows its feelings and expresses them openly. When it is hurt it cries. When it is angry it screams. When it is happy it smiles and laughs from deep down inside. This child is also highly sensitive and instinctual. It knows who to trust and who not to trust. This little child loves to play and to discover. Every moment is new and full of wonder. From this playfulness comes an inexhaustible well of creativity and aliveness.

As time goes on the child runs head-on into the demands of the adult world. The voice of grown-ups, with their own needs and wants, begins to drown out the inner voice of feelings and instincts. In effect, parents and teachers say, "Don't trust yourself, don't feel your feelings. Don't say this, don't express that. Do as we say, we know best."

With time those very qualities that gave the child its aliveness—curiosity, spontaneity, ability to feel—are forced into hiding. In the process of raising, disciplining, and educating children, adults often turn the child into a predictable adult. By eradicating the child's vulnerability (along with its lack of control), they severely damage the essential self of the child. The baby is thrown out with the bathwater. The adult world is not a safe place for children. For survival's sake, the growing youngster sends its delightful child spirit underground and locks it away. But that *Inner* Child never grows up and never goes away. It remains buried alive, waiting to be set free.

The Inner Child is constantly trying to get our attention, but many of us have forgotten how to listen. When we ignore our true feelings and gut instincts, we are ignoring the Inner Child. When we fail to nurture our body and soul, we neglect the Child Within. When we talk ourselves out of childlike needs with the excuse that they are not rational or practical—not the adult thing to do—we abandon the Inner Child. For instance, we may feel an impulse to skip for joy through the park, or to cry uninhibitedly over the loss of a friend. That is the Inner Child wanting to come out. But when the serious grown-up in us says, "No, you can't do that! Big boys don't cry. You must appear to be in control," the Inner Child gets locked in the closet.

When our Inner Child is blocked, we are robbed of our natural spontaneity and zest for life. Over time this may lead to low energy, chronic or serious illness. When our Inner Child is hidden we also separate ourselves from others. They never get to see our true feelings and wishes; they never see who we really are. This makes it impossible to experience true intimacy with others. We never get to truly know each other. What a tragedy and loss this is. **For us to be fully human, the Child Within must be embraced and expressed.**

No, I'm scared - No. No, I'm scared. No, I'm Scared. No, I'm scared
No, I'm scared. No. No, I'm scared. No. No, I'm Scared. No, I'm Scared.

ONE

"A Little Child Shall Lead Them"

Inside every adult, there is a child crying, "Let me out."

Who is this child living within? Why is it trapped inside? What does it have to offer? How can it be liberated? You will answer these questions for yourself as you do this book. I say *do* rather than *read* because this is a hands-on approach. Through a combination of words, pictures, and activities you will be guided in discovering, nurturing, and protecting your own Inner Child. My goal is to help you love your Inner Child and invite it to be a part of your life.

The concept of the Inner Child is not new. It actually has roots in ancient mythology and fairy tales. Virtually all religions have told stories of the child who becomes a savior or leader. The child is usually orphaned, abandoned, or its life is threatened. Moses was found abandoned in the bull rushes. Jesus was born in the humblest setting because "there was no room at the inn." His life was threatened by King Herod's slaughter of the infants. Similarly, Krishna's birth was accompanied by great danger. King Kansa had been told that the man who would eventually kill him was about to be born, so he consequently decreed that all newborn males be slain.

In Greek mythology the child Zeus was in danger of being devoured by his father Chronos. And as the father of Dionysius, Zeus was absent when his son was being torn to pieces by the Titans. The twins in Roman mythological lore, Romulus and Remus, were abandoned and set adrift on the river Tiber. European fairy tales also abound with child heroes who are threatened by ogres and demons: Hansel and Gretel had their witch, Cinderella had her wicked step-mother and nasty step-sisters, Jack had his giant, and Little Red Riding Hood had the wolf.

In this century, psychologist C. G. Jung and mythologist Joseph Campbell have shown us that these myths and legends have widespread appeal because they illustrate universal human experiences. For instance, all human beings have one thing in common: we all start out as vulnerable, dependent infants. Therefore, we can all resonate with the helpless, misunderstood, and abused children in these stories. Who has not experienced some kind of physical or emotional mistreatment in childhood?

The very nature of childhood leaves the infant or youngster open to harm. Insensitive or violent adults can certainly appear as giants, witches, and ogres in the eyes of a child. That is why the classic fairy tales hold our rapt attention time and time again, whether they are told from memory, read from a picture book, or portrayed on the screen. Walt Disney was well aware of this when he chose the story of Snow White for his first feature-length animated film. Even though he was scoffed at by financiers, he would not be deterred. He knew that the public would respond to this classic story in a new medium. His success rested on his ability to speak to the child in us all.

In many cultures we find this theme: the endangered child who must remain in obscurity and undergo trials until his true heroic nature is revealed. Jung saw the child as an archetype, a universal symbol existing within the collective unconscious. In his essay "The Psychology of the Child Archetype," he wrote:

> It is . . . not surprising that so many of the mythological saviours are child gods. This agrees exactly with our experience of the psychology of the individual, which shows that the "child" paves the way for a future change of personality. In the individuation process, it anticipates the

figure that comes from the synthesis of conscious and unconscious elements in the personality. It is therefore a symbol which unites the opposites; a mediator, bringer of healing, that is, one who makes whole. Because it has this meaning, the child motif is capable of numerous transformations. . . . I have called this wholeness that transcends consciousness the "self." The goal of the individuation process is the synthesis of the self.

Jung's words "the child paves the way for a future change of personality," and his reference to the child as "bringer of healing . . . one who makes whole" echos the biblical prophecy, "And a little child shall lead them."

Since the 1960s the Inner Child has become a popular theme in psychology. The Inner Child is that part of us who feels like a child and may cause us to behave in a childlike or childish way. Hugh Missildine wrote about it in his groundbreaking book, *Your Inner Child of the Past.* The Child state is also an important aspect of Transactional Analysis, which was developed by Eric Berne in the sixties and popularized in the seventies. Berne presented us with a picture of the inner world made up of a parent self, a child self, and an adult self. The parent self sets out the rules and regulations (the shoulds and the oughts). The child self feels and reacts. The adult thinks, makes decisions, and solves problems.

The 1980s saw the development of still another model in which the Inner Child plays an important role: Voice Dialogue. Developed by psychologists Hal Stone and Sidra Winkelman, Voice Dialogue demonstrates that the psyche is peopled by countless sub-personalities such as the Child, Critic, Pusher or Taskmaster, Protector, Beach Bum, Artist, Playboy or Playgirl, etc. The goal is to develop an *aware* ego at the center whose job is to be conscious of the sub-personalities. Like the director of a play, the aware ago decides which sub-personality will be allowed on stage at any given time. It must also be aware of which "actors" are lurking around backstage (the disowned or *shadow* selves, as Jung called them). In Voice Dialogue the goal is to be conscious of and accept all of our sub-personalities, allowing them appropriate expression. The Inner Child is often one of the disowned selves, one that we left behind as we grew to adulthood. As a trained Voice Dialogue facilitator, I have integrated this method into my work in art therapy and journal process. It provides an excellent framework for re-parenting the Inner Child.

The Inner Child also received recognition in the 1980s as part of the rapidly growing recovery movement. Treatment for addictive behavior is being addressed more and more in hospitals and rehabilitation centers. Much of this treatment includes work with the roots of addiction in childhood. Twelve-step programs applying the principles of Alcoholics Anonymous and Alanon (for co-dependents affected by alcoholism) have now been extended to include the Adult Children of Alcoholics. This program has now been broadened to support Adult Children from any type of dysfunctional family. Experts have estimated that ninety-five percent of the population received inadequate parenting. This may explain why programs for Adult Children have gained such great popularity. Almost all of us have some Inner Child healing to do.

In recent years, one of the most articulate writers on the Inner Child has been Charles Whitfield, M.D. In his best-selling book, *Healing the Child Within,* Whitfield led the way toward acknowledging the role of the Inner Child in recovery from co-dependence and being an adult child of a dysfunctional family. At the same time, through media coverage, there has been a growing recognition of the rampant child abuse in our culture. For instance, it has been estimated that one out of every four adults suffered some kind of sexual abuse in childhood. Clinician Alice Miller has shed light on the childhood roots of dysfunctional adult behavior. Her deeply moving book *For Your Own Good: Hidden Cruelty in Child-Rearing and the Roots of Violence,* lays bare the shocking truth of widespread violence against children and how this affects them in later life.

Based on my experience as an early-childhood educator and art therapist, I have concluded that we cannot eradicate child abuse in our culture without healing the wounds of our own Inner Child. We will never cure the epidemic of child abuse in the *outer world* until we stop abusing the Child in our *inner world.*

But how does Inner Child healing pertain to someone who was not severely abused in childhood? I would propose that in order to survive in our world we have all denied the Child Within to one degree or another. And this is also abuse. It is virtually impossible to grow up in our era of addictions and crime, wars and threat of environmental devastation, without our Inner Child going underground. Our world is not safe for that sensitive, vulnerable part of ourselves. But as you will see throughout this book, the Inner Child is at the core of our being. As our *feeling self*, it brings us enthusiasm and energy. None of us can be whole, happy adults without bringing the Inner Child into our lives and thereby healing it.

How do we do this? How do we heal our Inner Child? First of all by recognizing and experiencing it. That will be our task in Chapter 2. When we meet our Inner Child we often discover that our childhood needs were not met—needs for love, safety, trust, respect, and guidance. The absence of these basic conditions may have brought about a state of chronic anxiety, fear, shame, anger, and despair in our Inner Child. Recurring emotional and physical problems in adulthood are a sign that the Inner Child is trying to speak.

When basic human needs go unfulfilled, the individual is at high risk for developing abusive behavior toward self and others, creating problems in virtually all areas of life. It is also a well-known fact that family violence sets up a chain reaction. Parents violate their children. When those children grow up and become parents they often abuse their own children, and so on. Addicts who become parents frequently have children who become addicts. The brand of addiction may change—an alcoholic mother may have a drug-addicted son—but the pattern is the same. Violence and addiction are a tragic downward spiral. They get handed down from one generation to the next and have become epidemic in our society.

As individuals, how can we build our adult world on the shaky foundations of a frightened and isolated child who never got its basic needs met? It can't be done. Sooner or later a crisis hits—an illness, divorce, career upheaval, or financial disaster—and the structure crumbles. The mask of the adult persona begins to crack. At this point, some individuals look inward to examine and reevaluate their lives. They may seek assistance from therapists and self-help books, or join support groups where it is safe to acknowledge the damaged Child Within.

If you identify with this scenario, let me suggest that you use this book as part of your own personal program of healing. Complement this work with a support group, a 12-step program, therapy, or workshops. Inner Child healing cannot be done in isolation. After all, that little Child Within has been alone long enough. It is essential that we all find companions along the way—other individuals who are committed to caring for their own Inner Child. A support system creates a foundation for truly loving relationships.

It is important to remember one thing, however. *Only you can re-parent your Inner Child.* No one can do it for you. Only you are responsible for knowing and meeting your Inner Child's needs. So if you have been looking for love in all the wrong places, for someone to take care of your Inner Child for you, this book can help. It can also help you stop rescuing other people's abandoned and abused Inner Children. *Re-parenting themselves is their responsibility.*

Experiencing the Inner Child

The term "Inner Child work" is used a great deal these days. Many therapists are including "Inner Child work" in their practice with groups and individuals. Workshops and books on the subject are plentiful. And yet in my lectures and seminars throughout North America, many people tell me they are struggling with Inner Child work. They have read countless books, written personal histories, and shared their childhood fears and traumas in therapy and support groups. Yet they are still confused and unable to *feel* their Inner Child and bring it into their everyday lives. Many have reported that they had their first true *experience* of the Inner Child at one of my workshops or while doing exercises in my earlier books. They are the ones who encouraged me to share these methods of Inner Child healing in a book.

It is one thing to *talk about* the Inner Child; it is another thing to consciously experience it as a real living presence. Unless we "become as little children," we will not be healed. Unless we enter into the Child state *in a safe setting,* the Child Within will remain isolated and alone. Unless we reclaim our childlike feelings, sensitivity, wonderment, and aliveness, our Inner Child will remain wounded.

How do we know that our Inner Child is present? When we have feelings. The Inner Child is the emotional self. It is where our feelings live. When you experience joy, sadness, anger, fear, or affection your Child Within is coming out. When you are truly feeling your feelings you are allowing your Inner Child to be. Your Child Within is also active when you are being playful, spontaneous, creative, intuitive, and surrendering to the spiritual self. The experience of these states is often referred to as "being in your Inner Child." When you share this state with others it is referred to as "coming from your Inner Child."

The activities in this book are designed to give you safe, *firsthand experiences of your Inner Child.* Through drawing, writing, creative arts, and play you will find the voice of the Child who lives within you. You will discover its needs and wishes. You will also learn to activate the loving Parent Within who can nurture and protect that Inner Child. For no child exists in a vacuum. Our Inner Child will automatically draw out either a positive, supportive Inner Parent or a negligent and critical one. Without awareness, we automatically repeat the kind of parenting we received as children. We parent ourselves the way we were parented. However, if we do not like the way we were parented, we do have a choice. We can change. We can create a loving connection between the members of our own Inner Family and heal the wounds of childhood. We can re-parent ourselves.

Psychologically, the Child is indeed "father to the man." *Recovery of your Inner Child is the way to begin anew and to heal your life.* As the often quoted phrase promises, "It's never too late to have a happy childhood." I know this from my own personal experience and from observing others who have successfully re-parented themselves.

Discovering My Own Inner Child

Before I had ever heard of "the child within," my Inner Child began crying out to me through a physical illness. She had been abandoned so long that the only way she could get my attention was through a condition that made it impossible for me to function at all. The symptoms were extreme exhaustion and disorientation. This was aggravated by a series of medical mistakes that began when my condition was incorrectly diagnosed. As a result, the pharmaceutical drugs that were prescribed led to a chain reaction of side-effects.

All along my Inner Child knew that I had a serious disease. But as is so often the case with children, she did not have the words to express what she knew deep down inside. When the doctors used long Latin names, treated me with clinical coldness, and prescribed still another drug, my Inner Child felt intimidated and went further underground. Secretly she was panicked. For a while I tried to ignore her promptings. I rationalized and excused the inadequate medical treatment I was receiving, trying to believe that the doctors knew what they were doing (even though the facts showed otherwise).

Meanwhile, I had begun keeping a journal. I also read some books that had a profound impact on me. The diary of Anaïs Nin showed me that writing out the inner world of feelings could actually affect one's outer life. At the same time, Carl Jung's *Man and His Symbols* inspired me to draw my feelings out in the journal. The art that poured forth at this time was clearly coming from the unconscious. It had a strangely mysterious quality, as though I was writing in a foreign tongue. It was filled with symbols that I did not understand intellectually, but which spoke directly to my soul. After these drawings I always felt better physically and emotionally.

In this early drawing, a child appears underground crouching in a fetal position. Her tears of sorrow are watering the roots of a tree in which a heart has been split in half by storms. But up high in the sky is a butterfly, a harbinger of new beginnings. When I did this drawing I had no idea what I was doing or why. The images appeared mysteriously on the page, as if my hand had done the drawing on its own, much like automatic writing. The symbols came from a very deep corner of the unconscious.

This self-reflective journal process led me into therapy. In my first session with therapist Bond Wright, I was formally introduced to my Inner Child in the context of Transactional Analysis. In role-playing I discovered that my Inner Child was filled with rage at the doctors who had misdiagnosed my

Aug. 13 - 1973

condition and almost medicated me to death. In another role-play I became a Nurturing Parent with my arms holding an imaginary baby. As I crooned a lullaby, I realized that the infant in my arms was me: a new self being born. This experience was deeply empowering! I knew that I would no longer submit myself to medical negligence and mistreatment. So when my therapist recommended a truly caring woman physician who practiced preventive medicine, I contacted her immediately. This was a major step forward in my healing.

In the next therapy session my Inner Child was encouraged to speak again, this time in writing. Bond sat me on the floor in front of a large pad of newsprint paper and put a fat kindergarten crayon in my non-dominant (left) hand. She instructed me to write a contract with myself on how to apply what I was learning in therapy to everyday life. As soon as I began printing with my awkward, unschooled left hand, I regressed to about age four or five. I felt like a very young child just learning to write. This is what my Inner Child scrawled:

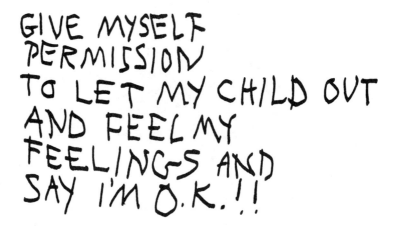

GIVE MYSELF PERMISSION TO LET MY CHILD OUT AND FEEL MY FEELINGS AND SAY I'M O.K.!!

I left the session feeling lighter and more energetic than I had in years. My Inner Child had finally been liberated and allowed to speak. It felt as if a huge burden had been lifted from my shoulders. After four years of personal crisis and the stress of juggling family, career, and everyone else's needs, I finally turned inward and embraced my own Inner Child. The cloud of heaviness and low energy I had been struggling with for months suddenly seemed to lift.

Getting in touch with my Inner Child in that session had a profound effect on my physical health. During the session my therapist recommended a physician, Dr. Louise Light, who she said practiced preventive medicine and educated her patients in self-care. Upon leaving the therapy session a child-like inner voice insisted that I call Dr. Light immediately. I stopped at a telephone booth and made an appointment to see Dr. Light on her first available opening. At my appointment with her a few days later, I found that she paid attention to my *feelings* as well as my physical condition, something that the other physicians had never done. She treated me with compassion and respect. My Inner Child could finally relax and feel safe.

Both Dr. Light and my therapist, Bond Wright, acknowledged the importance of journaling as part of my healing process. This validation of my discovery and my own experience had great meaning for me. My energy and enthusiasm for life began to return, and within a few weeks I felt well enough to resume work as an artist.

Thinking that I had been "cured," I excitedly started planning a new art project. No sooner had I begun, however, than the old pattern of self-criticism and self-pressure (which had contributed to my illness in the first place) resurfaced with a vengeance. As I was writing in my journal one day the voice of inner criticism began shouting in my head. "You've got to get back to work. You're not moving fast enough. You're not good enough. You'll fail. . . ." Without warning my left hand yanked the pen out of my right hand, drew this picture, and then scrawled a message:

What followed was a lively dialogue between my right hand and my left, between my Critical Inner Parent and a very assertive Child Within. As you will notice, the non-dominant handwriting appears in a different typeface. That will be the case throughout this book.

Left Hand: WHY ARE YOU SO IMPATIENT

Right Hand: Because I'm tired of waiting - feels like sitting in a rut -

Left Hand: BUT LOOK AT THE PAINTINGS WE'VE DONE. LIKE NOTHING THAT WENT BEFORE.

Right Hand: I know but it seems like so little. I feel so ignorant when I look around - all those other designers with all that technical skill - THIS IS PIG PARENT SPEAKING. YOU'RE SO STUPID - UNPRO-FESSIONAL CAN'T DO PERSPECTIVE DRAWING - DO SAME OLD THING - MOVE - GODDAMMIT MOVE - DO SOMETHING NEW - I WANT TO SHAKE YOU - HURRY UP

Left Hand: I HATE YOU WHEN YOU DO THIS. STOP PUTTING ME DOWN - STOP I'M BEAUTIFUL AND MY BEAUTY GROWS AND GROWS AND MY STRENGTH GROWS I AM ALWAYS GROWING UP THERE'S NOTHING THAT CAN STOP ME

Then my right hand wrote a commentary from the Observer Within:

Sitting in a rut feels like being shut in - in the dark - in the womb - waiting to be born into the light - waiting until the time comes naturally - not forcing, not pushing - just relaxing and letting life happen and letting me happen naturally

Right Hand: Sitting in a rut feels like
                      being shut in - in the dark -
                      in the womb - waiting to be
                      born into the light - waiting
                      until the time comes
                      naturally - not forcing,
                      not pushing - just relaxing
                      and letting life happen
                      and letting me happen
                      naturally

What a relief I felt after writing this dialogue. And what an incredible discovery! I had found the key for dealing with that tyrannical critical voice living within. It was like watching my own fairy tale. My Inner Child freed herself from the spell of the "wicked step-mother"—the Critical Parent within—by expressing her natural reaction to criticism and pressure. A beautiful feeling of calm welled up from within as I wrote the last passage with my dominant hand. I realized I had found my own fairy godmother—inside!

This dialogue between my right and left hand, between the Parent and Child, gave me a new perspective on my illness. In rereading the dialogue I was able to stand aside and witness the inner conflict. The inactivity of being sick in bed had felt like "sitting in a rut . . . shut in the dark." Suddenly, I understood the significance of my illness. It was part of being "born into the light." As I wrote the words "until the time comes naturally," and drew the little crouched fetus about to be born, there was a sudden shift. I could feel this loving and nurturing fairy godmother voice within coaching me through this rebirth. She spoke soothingly—"not forcing, not pushing—just relaxing and letting life happen and letting me happen naturally."

Of course, the inner Critical Parent had not been banished permanently. But now I had the tools for dealing with that nagging voice when it returned again. After acknowledging the critic, all I had to do was let my Inner Child express her feelings and know she was okay just the way she was.

Within a few weeks of this journal dialogue, I fully recovered from my illness. Incidentally, many years later the intuition of my Inner Child was confirmed regarding the nature of my condition. A diagnostician trained in iridology and sclerology informed me that I had been suffering with a life-threatening disease affecting the collagen, or connective tissue in the body. He also saw that I had recovered completely.

After resuming my career as a free-lance designer and artist, it became clear that my heart was no longer in that work. Perhaps it would be more accurate to say that my Inner Child had lost enthusiasm for the decorative and commercial art that I was doing. All she wanted to do was write and draw the inner world of feelings and intuition. Of course, my Critical Parent panicked, believing that such personal art and writing was ugly, a waste of time, and incapable of providing me with a livelihood. Fortunately, I turned up the volume on the Inner Child's voice and followed my heart right into a career as an art therapist.

As my private practice evolved, Inner Child healing became the core of my work. This was not by conscious design. It just happened that way. I kept finding that regardless who my clients were, or which workshop I was leading, all roads seemed to take us back to the Inner Child. So I developed the techniques that had been central to my own recovery, and showed others how to use them. These methods include drawing, writing, play, movement, drama, and creative activities with clay and other media. These are the same tools and techniques that you will be using in this book to re-parent yourself.

Tools for Re-Parenting the Inner Child

DRAWING

Those who have raised or educated children with awareness know that the creative arts are the natural language of the child. Given a healthy environment and the guidance of nurturing adults, children spontaneously express themselves through the arts. No one has to tell young children that creative expression is fun, and that it makes you feel good about yourself and the world. Pre-schoolers and kindergartners draw and paint, play with clay, build and construct, act, dance, and sing with great enthusiasm. They do not have to be coaxed or instructed.

When I was training teachers, my work included observing young children in classrooms throughout the United States, from inner-city ghettos to rural farm areas. These were children of all races and socioeconomic backgrounds: Asian and Hispanic refugees, blacks who had survived the Watts riots, farm workers, upper-middle-class suburbanites. No matter where these children were or what they looked like, they all had one thing in common: the language of art. This is no coincidence. Drawing comes before writing in a child's development. In fact, art therapy is used with children who cannot verbalize their feelings. What cannot be spoken can often be expressed more safely in art. And even if a child is articulate, sometimes words are not enough. Who can translate into words the precise meaning of a bold, black scribble? Watching a child release bottled-up rage or fear with crayons or clay is a profoundly moving experience.

It is no accident, then, that the *Inner* Child also expresses its feelings and needs more easily through art. In my workshops drawing has been one of the most direct and enjoyable ways of reaching the Inner Child. Drawing gets people out of their rational, analytical, adult frame of mind and immerses them in the Child state. We know that drawing comes predominantly from the right hemisphere of the brain. This is the side that seems to specialize in visual/spatial perception, as well as emotional and intuitive expression. What we often forget is that young children, by their very nature, are predominantly right-brained. That is why scribbling and drawing are so natural for them.

However, this enjoyment of right-brain, multisensory activity gets shut down through restrictive parenting and a left-brain school system that places an inordinate emphasis on verbal logic and memorization. With the exception of sports, right-brained learning modalities are the first to be dropped from school budgets. It is a well-known fact that the arts are the step-children of the curriculum. When the arts are eliminated from education, children lose one of their most powerful and enjoyable means of self-expression. As they "advance" through school, they are systematically forced to deny the voice of the Inner Child—the feeling, playful, creative self.

This brings us to another dilemma: the widely held belief that only a few are talented and capable of expressing through art, and that the rest of us should not even bother. This erroneous belief has robbed most people of their natural birthright: the ability to express the Inner Child through creative arts. The truth is that anyone can draw or, for that matter, express him or herself through movement, dance, music, etc.

It is the Critical Parent Within (the product of society's brainwashing) that stops us from engaging in art activities just for the fun of it. It is the Critic who says, "You'll make mistakes. You'll look stupid. You make ugly art. Heaven forbid!" Sounds like a parent or schoolteacher belittling a child, doesn't it? If this all sounds painfully familiar to you, if you have heard this battle in your own head, then take heart. In a later chapter, we deal with inner criticism and judgment that blocks us from letting the Child Within express itself. And you will be guided in simple drawing and art activities designed specifically to let your Inner Child out.

As you allow yourself to draw, in spite of self-doubts and inner criticism, you relearn the language of the child. For if you want to embrace your Inner Child, it is important to meet it halfway. The intellectual, verbally complex language of adults keeps us separate from our Child Heart. On the other hand, when we draw our feelings out, we are speaking the language of the Inner Child.

The following drawings of the Inner Child were done by adults attending my workshops.

WRITTEN DIALOGUES

In the early days of my art therapy practice, I shared with my clients the right/left-hand writing process that I had discovered in my journal work. It soon became clear that this technique helped *everyone* experience their Inner Child. They seemed to reach deeper levels of feelings, memories, and intuition than they did with art therapy alone. One explanation might be that the awkwardness and lack of control experienced when writing with the non-dominant hand actually puts us into the Inner Child state. Picture a young child just learning to make marks on paper, struggling to control the writing instrument. Many adults say that is exactly how they feel when first writing or drawing with their "other hand."

Now picture a slightly older child attempting to write words that "mean something," that communicate thoughts and feelings to others. For a youngster, this is a formidable challenge. Many adults regress to that experience when they begin writing with their unschooled hand. Their spelling and grammar resemble that of a little kid. This is even true of people who are highly educated and normally have very sophisticated verbal skills. It is obvious to me from watching this phenomenon so many times in workshops, with thousands of adults of all ages, that we are tapping into a part of the brain and a part of the psyche where the child lives.

Now there is often some resistance to writing with the non-dominant hand. We believe we cannot write with our "other" hand, so we never do it. We view the non-writing hand as retarded, and it is. It has had no training and practice. Our non-dominant hand has atrophied from lack of use, and has stayed frozen at a very early stage of development. The paradox is that it is this retarded "other hand" that can lead us back to our Inner Child.

There may also be some physiological reasons why the Inner Child speaks so naturally through the other hand. When I first began teaching this method, a student told me of a conversation she had had with Roger Sperry, a pioneer in right/left brain research. Upon telling Dr. Sperry about the creative and emotional expressiveness she was discovering through writing with her non-dominant hand, he responded: "You're opening up your right hemisphere." Sperry's comment stimulated in me an intense personal interest in brain research. I believe there are connections between brain research and Inner Child work, so I would like to discuss it briefly.

The Brain, the Hand, and the Inner Child

Each hemisphere of the human brain controls the opposite side of the body. It also appears that there are specialized functions for each half of the brain. The left brain contains language centers that control verbal and analytical processing. It has been described as the linear and logical side of the brain. By contrast, the right brain appears to be primarily non-verbal and governs visual/spatial perception, as well as emotional expression and intuition.

My observations show that writing with the non-dominant hand directly accesses right-brain functions. This phenomenon holds true for both right-handers and left-handers. As we will see, this hand expresses feelings much more directly and with greater force. It also taps into a deeper level of instinct and emotional memory, which are so important for healing the Inner Child. When we write dialogues between the Child (non-dominant hand) and the adult or Inner Parent (dominant hand), we seem to be conversing between the two hemispheres of the brain.

A different model of the brain, which seems to hold great promise for understanding these deeper levels of instinct and feeling, is the Triune Brain Theory, developed by Dr. Paul D. MacLean (formerly chief of the National Institute of Mental Health Laboratory for Brain Evolution). MacLean's theory describes three separate but intimately connected brains, each successively nestled within the other, which reflect distinct stages of human evolution.

The oldest and deepest part of the brain, the *Reptilian Brain*, corresponds anatomically to the R-complex (medulla, pons, and spinal cord). It governs

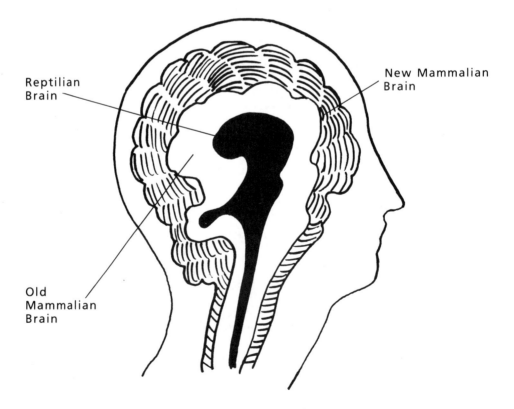

survival instincts such as food finding, mating, defending one's territory, and habitual behavior. The next layer to develop was the *Old Mammalian Brain* (Limbic System), which is the seat of *emotions*. It also receives and processes sensory input and communicates it to the other two brains. The youngest and outermost layer of the brain is the Neocortex, or the *New Mammalian Brain*. It is the "thinking cap" and controls abstract reasoning.

Much of psychotherapy has been done at this outer level of the Neocortex. These are the analytical and "talk" therapies. But as so many of us have found, these modalities do not reach the Inner Child. It could take years. The Inner Child speaks much more readily in the language of feelings: body movement, play, and the arts. When the Inner Child does use words, they are simple and direct and full of feeling.

Recently psychologist Álvaro López-Watermann has developed a theory based on his dream research correlating these evolutionary layers of the brain with distinct states of psychological experience. (His model adds a fourth brain, the *Peiskian Brain,* corresponding anatomically with the pineal gland.) According to López-Watermann, when consciousness identifies with a particular part of the brain (Peiskian, Reptilian, Old Mammalian, or New Mammalian), it produces a corresponding state—transcendental, abstract dream, dream, or waking. (Every night our psyche experiences the cycle of the first three states while sleeping.) The activity of each of the four brains can be thought of as a semi-autonomous psychological entity. López-Watermann refers to these corresponding parts of the psyche as the *Regulator, Governor, Supportive (Emotional) Mind,* and *Intellect.* According to his theory, the language of the *Supportive Mind* is memory-images and feelings. It may be that when we experience the Inner Child state, this deeper and older emotional part of the brain (the Supportive Mind) is being brought into dominance.

Our present dilemma is that this deeper emotional part of the brain often becomes sealed off from our conscious awareness. Recent research shows that there are "gating" mechanisms that inhibit memory of painful early experiences. For survival's sake, the feeling Inner Child goes into the closet and the door is shut. Healing happens when we open the door and invite the Inner Child to come out and be a part of our lives. This is done in a safe atmosphere with respect and protection for that tender being. The techniques in this book are designed to help you create that safe atmosphere of trust so essential for healing your Inner Child.

One of the writing techniques you will be using most frequently is dialoguing with both hands. In these conversations you will ask questions with the dominant hand, the one you normally write with. And your Inner Child will respond through the non-dominant hand, the one you usually do not use for writing. As you see in the fragments of dialogues below, the Child speaks in its own voice: simple, to the point, and often charged with feeling.

Who are you?
BABY
How do you feel?
LIKE CRYIN - I TIRED
OF WORK ALL THE
TIME-

Who are you?
I'M ME
How do you feel?
SILLY - I WANT
TO PLAY

What is your name?
NANCY
How old are you?
2 ½
What do you like to do?
Play with my friends

Who are you?
I am angel
How do you feel?
I feel light & airy
I live in the clouds
I am what you see
when you look in the
sky on a cloudy day —
I am fluffy & playful.

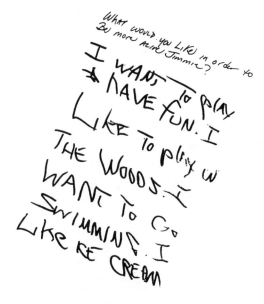

You will also notice that the style of the dominant hand's writing is visually quite different from that of the non-dominant hand. This is to be expected. Through training and practice, our *dominant hand* developed manual dexterity, strength, and control. The "other hand," which was neglected, looks awkward, weak, and childlike.

In dialogues written with both hands, the skilled dominant hand speaks for the adult as well as our parental voices. Psychologically, this is perfectly understandable. It is the very nature of these adult and parental voices to value skill and control. In doing these dialogues the Critical Parent often becomes extremely frustrated with the slow and sloppy writing of the non-dominant hand (Inner Child). Like an impatient parent, the dominant hand will try to control the situation by yanking the pen away so it can speak for the Inner Child. Its attitude is that it knows best and can write better and faster. This occurrence mirrors what has happened to the Inner Child in our lives—it has been dominated and controlled by our impatient and critical Inner Parent.

The problem is that this impatient parental self *does not know* how the Inner Child feels and therefore cannot speak for it. In these dialogues penmanship, spelling, and grammar are unimportant. It's the *feelings* that count. Try to listen to what the Child is saying and enjoy its precious little voice. You may be surprised at what it has to tell you!

If a critical reaction to your Inner Child's writing comes up, simply notice it. This is just your Critical Parent speaking. (We will deal more with the Critical Parent in Chapter 8.) Allow the Inner Child to keep writing with your non-dominant hand. One of the most beneficial aspects of right/left hand dialoguing is that it gives you a tangible experience of how you have been treating your Inner Child. With this new awareness you now have a choice to stay with the status quo or to change your ways and begin to honor the Child Within.

Play and Creative Activities

It is a well-known fact that children develop and learn through play. While playing they explore, test their limits, and develop skills. Allowed to play without pressure and criticism, children's true creativity blossoms from within. Watch any group of nursery school kids or kindergartners. Left to their own devices they will play with finger paints and clay, scribble with crayons, erect entire cities with building blocks, create magical castles and landscapes in the sandbox, and invent their own world through dramatic play with costumes and props.

Metaphors are natural to children. They adore make-believe. The youngest children create scenarios and act them out. They can turn anything into a prop. A broom handle becomes a sword. A garbage can lid becomes a shield, and a packing crate becomes a fort. No one has to teach children the fun of creative play. It is an intrinsic human ability that shows itself best in the child. On the contrary, society teaches children to *stop* being creative, to grow up, and to be "practical." If the Inner Child is to be fully reclaimed, this innate creativity must be allowed to express itself. This creative aspect of the Inner Child is often called the Magical Child (to be discussed in Chapter 10).

The expressive arts have a great deal to offer in healing the Inner Child. Creative activities done for the sheer joy of the experience (without pressure to perform) inevitably allow us to revive the Inner Artist that we lost in growing up. The enrichment of our lives that results from this bursting forth of the Creative Child is so far-reaching as to be almost beyond words. You must experience it to believe it.

Interwoven throughout this book you will find playful activities for bringing out that delightful child/artist within who is full of wonderment, curiosity, and joy. You will get to put adulthood aside for periods of time while you experiment with crayons, clay, and other simple art materials. There will also be time to dance and move spontaneously from your Inner Child, to role-play, and to explore the mysterious world of your dreams.

At this point your Critical Parent may rear up its head and say to your Inner Child, "You can't paint. You can't draw. You don't have any talent. And anyway, I don't want you making a mess around here." If this happens just observe it. But do not let your Critical Parent stop you. If it becomes obstinate, have faith. You will learn to deal with the voice of criticism in a later chapter.

The most important thing to keep in mind is that these playful and creative activities are the Inner Child's natural realm. You are not imposing anything foreign or strange upon yourself. You are simply allowing your Inner Child to speak a forgotten language. Creative expression is the Child's true mother tongue; all children understand and speak it. This is your human heritage. Reclaim it. Experience for yourself what Joseph Campbell described as "the rapture of being alive." This is the gift your Inner Child has to give you.

MATERIALS

Plain white paper (Xerox or computer paper)
Newsprint paper (18" x 24")
Felt pens (assorted colors)
Crayons (assorted colors)
Wet ceramic clay (hard work surface such as masonite or wood)
Scissors
Grocery bag
Personal calendar
Magazines with photos
Glue
Finger paints
Recorded music and sound system
Tape recorder and tape
You may wish to do the exercises in a notebook, sketchbook, or blank journal.
Feel free to draw with colored pencils or pastels instead of felt pens or crayons if
    you wish.

GUIDELINES

You can do the exercises in this book whenever you want, whenever you have something to work on with yourself. It is not necessary to work on this material every day; however, the more you do it, the more you will benefit. If it's suitable, set aside a special time each day, such as just before falling asleep. Keep a notebook and try to keep your entries in chronological order. It's a good idea to read this book one chapter at a time, in order to digest the material. Then do the exercises and continue on to the next chapter. If your style is to skim the entire book first to get an overview, then go back and do the exercises, that's fine; just don't expect to read and do all the exercises in one sitting.

Safety is essential, whether you are healing the Inner Child with the guidance of a professional, in a self-help support group, or on your own. Creating a home for the Child requires that you welcome it into an atmosphere that is safe.

When using this book as a guide to recovery of your Inner Child, it is very important *to keep your work confidential.* This is especially true when getting to know your *Vulnerable* Child. That is not to say that you cannot share certain portions of your work. But if you do, be highly selective. Share only with those who are supportive of your healing process and of you, such as your therapist, a trusted member of your support group, etc. If your Vulnerable Child feels safe with your spouse, lover, or best friend, sharing might be appropriate. If you have any doubts about who to share with, ask your Vulnerable Child. Do a right/left-hand dialogue. Ask the Child if it feels okay about sharing any of your work with this person or that one. Ask how much you should share and what specific content. Your Inner Child will let you know.

Do not share with individuals who are judgmental of you and try to control your feelings, thoughts, or behavior. It is foolish and destructive to expose the Inner Child to that type of energy or attitude. Highly opinionated people who are not receptive to who you are, and adults who are out of touch with their own Inner Child, cannot understand this kind of healing work. If you share your process with them, you will certainly be opening yourself to more damage of the Child Within.

In later chapters you will be given tools for providing healthy protection for your Inner Child. As you strengthen your Nurturing Parent Within as well as the Inner Protective Parent, the Child will feel stronger because it has both safety and support. Paradoxically, the little Child Within leads us to our true power. This is not power *over* others, nor control and manipulation. Rather, it is the power of the Inner Self, which is synonymous with our Higher Power or Higher Self. I prefer the term Inner Self because it reminds me that this power resides within, not on some remote mountaintop or far away in some unreachable heaven.

The Inner Child resides in the heart. As we open our heart to our own Inner Child, we open our heart to all. And that is how we find the source of our true power: love.

TWO

Meeting Your Inner Child

Direct experience of the Inner Child happens in many ways. It is something we all have at one time or another, but may not have recognized. I call this experience of the Child Within the "Child state." When you enter the Child state, you feel and behave like a child. You may even be unaware of it yourself, but others often notice. They see it in your face, eyes, or body; they hear it in your voice. They also observe it in your behavior.

Often, when adults speak about experiences of the Inner Child, they inadvertently place their hands over their belly or heart. Although this gesture is often unconscious, it is a way of acknowledging the Child's presence in the body. Our Inner Child speaks through bodily sensations. It reacts emotionally when we experience physical pain. It may feel physical pain in response to strong emotions. When we are tired and want a nap, are under the weather, or feel very ill, that is the Inner Child asking us to take care of it. In the first encounter with my Inner Child in therapy, the therapist told me afterward that my facial expression and body language had the qualities of a little kid: spontaneous and awkward. In the Child state, I was unaware of how I looked. Not until later when she gave me that feedback did I become conscious of my appearance. For imitating or "acting like a child" had been the farthest thing from my mind. This was no pretense. I had actually "become as a little child." There is an immense difference between *pretending* to be a child and *experiencing* the Child Within. The Child state comes from inside. It is a feeling in the body and emotions. It has nothing to do with performing or play-acting. In fact, you can experience your Inner Child without moving an inch or saying a word.

There are many activities ahead that are designed to help you find that Child, nurture it, and include it in your life. But you can start right now to become aware of the Inner Child in your daily life. Since the Inner Child is very physical, it may come out when you are enjoying sports, or dancing, or simply walking delightedly along a sandy beach at sundown listening to the whoop of sea gulls overhead. Your Child may tell you it wants a tall

glass of lemonade on a hot summer afternoon, or a big container of crunchy popcorn at the movies, or a steaming bowl of soup on a cold winter evening.

Sometimes the Inner Child wants to cuddle up under a soft blanket for an afternoon nap; at other times your Child may want to have fun hiking in the mountains. It may want to "play dress-up" and wear wild colors or glitzy jewelry. Other times it may prefer messing around in the garden in old jeans, a paint-spattered shirt, and floppy hat. Some Inner Children thrive on ball games, while others would rather have a tea party. Stop for a moment and reflect upon some of the physical ways in which your Inner Child comes out in your life.

When we stay exclusively in the grown-up world of thoughts, plans, and responsibilities, we cut ourselves off from our bodies. This is often referred

to as living in our heads. Living in our heads, away from our bodies, is one way that we abandon the Inner Child. So begin paying special attention, on a daily basis, to the Inner Child who lives in your body.

One way to become more aware of the physicality of the Inner Child is to observe children in the outer world. Watch their movement, observe how they interact with the environment with their whole bodies.

Another place the Inner Child lives is in our emotions. When we have feelings, our Inner Child is speaking to us privately. We do not have to express those feelings outwardly in order to know they are there. Feeling something, even if we do not have a name for it, is an experience of the Child state. The activities in this book were designed to help you become aware of your Inner Child feelings.

When we *express* our feelings, that is when the Child comes out. We can do this alone or with others. This may happen through body language, facial expressions, or physical movement. Or the Child might slip out in sounds or speech. When my Inner Child came out for the first time in therapy, she spoke with a lisp. This is not surprising. I actually had a lisp as a little kid, but it gradually "disappeared" due to repeated admonishment from adults.

Sometimes when a bilingual or bicultural person's Inner Child comes out it writes in a "foreign" language—the mother tongue, the language of the home and of early experiences. These written dialogues may come out in the mother tongue, even if the person never learned to *write* that language. Regressing to the Inner Child state brings recall of early experiences that were apparently encoded in the brain in the mother tongue. Therefore it is understandable that the Inner Child would write about those experiences in that early language. Of course, the spelling and grammar are often incorrect, but the words and the meaning come through loud and clear.

Another place we are likely to encounter the Inner Child is in moments of spontaneity and adventure. The Inner Child thrives on play. It loves to explore and create, to experiment with new ways of doing things. Its innocence and lack of old, encrusted beliefs and concepts allow it to live each moment, each day, as a new discovery.

The Inner Child lives in our imagination, in the rich world of fantasy and make-believe where our creativity is rooted. It is the Child in us that sparks that creative flame in whose absence life becomes repetitive, dull, and boring. For children are *not* dull and boring. Grown-ups? Yes, very often. But children, no. It is their aliveness in the moment, their ability to simply *be* (without goals, without agendas), that gives children so much vitality. And it is the same with our *Inner* Child.

In your everyday life, observe children wherever possible: in the supermarket, on the street, maybe even in your own home or classroom. Watch what they do, listen to what they say. Be with them without judgment, without having to change them. They will teach you about your Inner Child, in case you have forgotten.

Also, begin to notice signs of the Inner Child in other adults. How do you notice that there is a healthy Child alive inside another grown-up? What are the signs that an Inner Child has been stifled or is running rampant?

If you observe children who are not getting their needs met—the needs for love, attention, guidance, and care—you will get an insight into what happens to an *Inner* Child whose needs are not met. Crankiness, irritability, and temper tantrums are a sure sign that the Inner Child is disturbed. It may need more sleep, less pressure from the Parent self, more play time, or quiet time alone. The Inner Child may need firm guidance if it has gotten out of hand through behaviors that are childish instead of childlike. If we do not understand our Inner Child, its craving for love and attention may be misinterpreted. Instead of listening to its feelings, we feed it too much food. Instead of play time, we give it drugs. Instead of self-love, we give it sex at the wrong time or with inappropriate partners.

This pattern of substitutes was painfully clear in the case of Alexandra, one of my clients. A young woman in her early twenties, Alexandra had three years' sobriety from cocaine addiction. She had been troubled with low energy, depression, and difficulty in relationships. In a therapy session, I asked to talk to her Inner Child. Alexandra got up from her chair, curled up in a ball on the floor, and became her Inner Child. She looked very forlorn.

We sat quietly for a while. When the Inner Child felt safe with me, we conversed. She said she felt very sad and had a lot of feelings that Alexandra did not want to hear about. I then asked her if this had been going on for a long time. "Yes," she replied. "A long time. It used to be that when I came out, when I had feelings, she gave me drugs to shut me up. She gave me cocaine." As she learned to re-parent herself, to listen to her feelings and respond to her Inner Child's needs, Alexandra was able to rebuild her life. A few years later she had children of her own and was able to be a very competent mother because she had learned to be a parent to her own Inner Child.

It is very common for an abandoned Inner Child to cry out for help through illness. That was certainly true in my own case. And I have seen this pattern over and over in my work with people who have life-threatening diseases (AIDS and cancer) as well as chronic illness (Epstein-Barr virus and Chronic Fatigue Syndrome). It is during times of illness that the Inner Child is the most vulnerable and most desperately in need of love and compassion.

Any area of our lives where there is chronic pain and dissatisfaction may be signaling us that an Inner Child needs help. Beyond the generally recognized addictions, there are other symptoms of a neglected Inner Child: obsessive worry and fear, addiction to rage and criticism, and accident-proneness. Co-dependency or compulsive rescue/control of others is a sure sign that one's own Inner Child has been neglected while the Inner Parent focuses on the Inner Child of others. Chronic depression, boredom, or crippling creative blocks (especially debilitating for professionals in the arts) may also be evidence that the Inner Child is seriously wounded.

Throughout this book, you will be given tools for identifying the many faces of the Inner Child: the Vulnerable Child and the Angry Child, as well as the Playful, Creative, and Spiritual Child Within. As you experience and re-parent the wounded Child, the magical and joyful child will also emerge to heal your life.

One homework assignment that I give everyone who attends my Inner Child workshops is to see the movie *Big*. The hero, Josh, is eleven years old. He is tired of being pushed around because of his size and not being taken seriously because he is a kid. Frustrated by being in that awkward state between childhood and adolescence, Josh wishes he could be big. Little Josh gets his wish and wakes up the next morning in the big body of Tom Hanks. I feel that Big Josh as portrayed by Hanks is the ultimate portrait of an Inner Child in an adult body. I have heard that Hanks hung out with a real kid for a considerable amount of time while preparing to play this role. He did a masterful job because he contacted his own Inner Child and simply let him out. He did not have to "act" frightened, silly, playful, creative, and vulnerable. All he had to do was *be in his Inner Child.* That is why Hanks was totally believable in the part.

I have seen the film many times and will undoubtedly see it again. It is some of the best Inner Child therapy I know. If you have not seen it, I urge you to do so. Believe me, your Inner Child will thank you. If you have a hard time accessing your own Inner Child, I would suggest that you rent this video at once. Better than all the psychological descriptions and clinical definitions, *Big* captures the essence of the Inner Child.

Before embarking on the journey to meet your own Inner Child, there are some important things to keep in mind. The first thing is trust-building. The adult world is not safe for little children. Adults can be careless, thoughtless, and cruel toward children. If we have behaved badly toward our Inner Child, it may not trust us. It may not want to come out at first. Or it may come out slowly, with ambivalence and hesitation. If that is the case, relax and slow down. This will take time and patience. It will also require faith that the gap can be bridged, that the Child's wounds can be healed. Others who have gone before you have healed the relationship with their Inner Child. I have included these examples from students, clients, and readers of my other books to provide inspiration. They tell their stories and share their pictures and dialogues in the pages that follow.

As you learn to re-parent yourself, you can build trust by approaching the Inner Child with respect, acceptance, open-mindedness, and love. This is a child you are meeting. Let it feel and speak as a child. Let it draw and write like a child. Nothing will shut communication down faster than precon-ceived adult ideas about who the Inner Child is, who it "should" be, what it "should" feel and say, and how it "ought" to think. The exercises you will be doing in this book were designed to help you make it safe for your Inner Child to come out. If it is not safe, the Child simply will go back into hiding. It has a right to do that. In fact, sometimes that is necessary for its survival. The more open you are to hearing its needs and the more willing you are to *invite* it to dialogue with you, the more likely it will be to come out and meet you.

Respecting your Inner Child means allowing it to be whatever it is. It may appear as a boy or as a girl. It may have a name or it may have no name. Sometimes the names change. One day your Inner Child may have a nick-name from your own childhood, another day it might have a name you have never heard before. Its age may change as well. One day it may be three years of age, another day an infant, and another day a five-year-old. If you try to be rational or analytical about these things, the Inner Child will either shut down or tell you off (as you will see in several dialogues that appear later on). Like all children, the Inner Child has a different sense of time and a very different set of priorities than the adult self. It values feelings, play, creativity, imagination, symbols, and the soul. It opens the door to the essential, eternal, timeless Inner Self or Higher Power, as we will see later on.

The first activity is a meeting with your Inner Child. Find a quiet, safe place where you can be alone without distraction. You will also need some materials. Check the list at the beginning of the exercise and make sure you have your supplies handy. And, of course, the most important ingredient in this and all other meetings with your Inner Child is an OPEN MIND and an OPEN HEART.

MEETING THE CHILD WITHIN

MATERIALS: Crayons and paper.

1. You are about to meet with your Inner Child. Sit quietly and picture in your mind's eye a beautiful place where the two of you can visit in your imagination. Be sure it is a place that is safe and comfortable for your Inner Child. It might be out in nature surrounded by trees and flowers, or near water or mountains. Or you can imagine a warm, cozy room.

2. Close your eyes and go to this place. In your imagination, picture your Inner Child there, spend a few moments with him or her.

3. With your non-dominant hand draw a picture of your Inner Child. Take your time and let this drawing unfold from your Inner Child. Do not plan it or try to picture the outcome in advance. It may feel awkward and slow. Just be patient. This is your Inner Child speaking through pictures, a language of the heart and the innermost Self.

The process of drawing your Inner Child probably shed a great deal of light upon your relationship with that little being inside you. Stop and reflect for a moment on what the experience was like. Did you criticize yourself for the manner in which your Child drew the picture (with your non-dominant hand)? Did you berate your Child for having no talent or artistic skill? Or did you relax and have fun allowing your Inner Child to be itself and draw in its own style?

Look at the finished drawing. How do you feel about it? What does the Child in the picture seem to be saying to you? On a separate piece of paper with your dominant hand write down any reactions or comments about the drawing.

In a workshop, Maria did this drawing of her Inner Child. Later she wrote about the experience and gained some important insights about her childhood and her healing process.

Here is what Maria wrote about the process:

> Being left-handed, I did the exercise with my right hand. I started to write, "I have been discovered," because I had just discovered that my lifelong depression was due to my upbringing in a dysfunctional family. I am the seventh child in a family of thirteen. My mother chose me to help her raise her other children. I feel as though I didn't exist. I've suffered depression all my life. Needless to say, I was shocked to find that I had written in "I have been *recovered*." As I started to draw, the number 8 is what appeared on the page. I can't help thinking that perhaps that is when my life ended. This exercise has given me much hope.

If you wish, you can go on with the next activity at this time. It is a technique for finding out more about your Inner Child by talking directly with it. If you prefer to wait until another time, then put the picture where you can look at it frequently. You will be needing it again, so keep it in a safe place until you are ready to do the next exercise, TALKING WITH YOUR INNER CHILD.

TALKING WITH YOUR INNER CHILD

MATERIALS: Crayons, paper, and Inner Child drawing from previous exercises.

1. Look at the drawing of the Inner Child that you did in the last exercise. Write out a conversation using both hands. You, as the Adult, will write with your dominant hand (the hand you normally write with); your Inner Child will write or print with the "other" (non-dominant) hand. Open the conversation by telling the child you want to get to know it so that you can take better care of it. Ask for its name and anything else it wants to tell you about itself: age, how it feels, what it likes and doesn't like, and what it wants from you.

2. Ask your Inner Child to draw a picture of what it wants most at this time in your life.

3. Close the conversation by asking the Child to tell you anything else it wants you to know. Thank the Child for coming out and expressing itself. Tell it that you want to have more of these talks so you can get to know it better.

4. Put both pictures someplace where you can look at them frequently. Use them as a reminder of the presence of your Inner Child in your life.

Michelle did the following drawing and dialogue in a workshop. Afterward she found a childhood snapshot of herself in cowgirl costume sitting on a pony. This was the same image her Inner Child drew in its own simple way with her non-dominant hand.

Adult: Who are you?

Child: I'm Shelly.

Adult: How do you feel?

Child: I'm neat. I'm sitting on my horse.

Adult: Tell me about yourself.

Child: I'm back when you knew you were perfect. I'm full of fun & I like to run.

Adult: What happened to you?

Child: I don't know. I went away & I don't play.

Adult: What would you like me to do for you?

Child: You need to remember & honor me.

Kathy did dialogues with her Inner Child over a period of months. This process brought such lightness to her life that she looked physically different—younger, happier, more open.

Katy

Adult: Who are you?

Child: I call myself Katy. You know who I am—I am inside you. I am you.

Adult: Kathy, what's it feel like to be you?

Child: You called me Kathy. My name is Katy! I can't talk to you if you don't use my right name. KATY. If yo call me something else, I won't talk to you.

Adult: Ok, Katy, I'm sorry.

Child: That's better. I can't come out if you don't say my name right.

Adult: Katy, how old are you?

Child: 2½ or tree.

Adult: What does it feel like to be that old?

Child: I like it we want to stay here.

Adult: Katy, who else is there?

Child: Friends. I have friends with me all the time. They're inside.

Adult: Can you tell me about your friends, Katy? Who are they?

Child: They are like me but not. They talk to me an keep me company. We play together.

Adult: What do you play?

Child: We play make up and pretend. We play with our babys—we have a cat named angel, 2 doggies—little black ones Scottie and Lassie—a baby Hippo—Henrietta. Then there's 2 other doggies with wrinkles. Bonnie and Clyde and the bunnies Beetrice & Ginger and Elina & her babies Katrina & Cosmo. Here I am with my friends.

Adult: Kathy

Child: You called me that again.

Adult: I was just going to ask you Katy, how do you like big people?

Child: I won't talk to them.

Adult: But you're talking to me.

Child: Your different. Not like those other ones.

This next drawing of an Inner Child was done by Anne Leigh Courtney. (Anne also did the drawing of the hidden Inner Child at the beginning of Chapter 1.) This drawing and dialogue between Anne and her Inner Child ends with a touching expression of love from a Nurturing Parent Voice (which we will explore in a later chapter).

Adult: What's your name?

Child: My name is Annie.

Adult: How old are you?

Child: I am six.

Adult: I'd like to get to know you better Annie. What do you like to do?

Child: I like to play. I like to visit Mr. Tree. I like hugs and splashing my feet in puddles.

Adult: What don't you like?

Child: I don't like mean people.

Adult: What would you like me to do for you?

Child: I like you to LOVE ME, be gentle with me and pay attention to me.

Adult: I love you Annie. I love you very much. I am here to take care of you, give you hugs and protect you from mean people. I'm glad you are here. I love you. Love, Annie.

Although this next woman reported that she had some difficulty feeling connected with her Inner Child, she had begun the process of letting the Child speak. That is all it takes to start re-parenting yourself. Remember, it is an ongoing adventure of personal renewal.

Happy. Happy. Happy. I am perfect. I am a doll. I am not real.

Can you reach any feelings that seem real?

Adult: Who are you?

Child: I'm you when you were a young child. I am your inner child.

Adult: How do you feel?

Child: I feel like swinging. I will swing. See Tova swing. swing. swing. swing. Don't get my dress dirty. I am pretty. pretty pretty, pretty. Such a happy child. Happy. Happy. Happy. I am perfect. I am a doll. I am not real.

Adult: Can you reach any feelings that seem real?

Child: I will collapse in a puddle. I will melt if I feel. I will be a blob. I will die. Maintain the armor all the time is just too difficult. I've got to get out of here out of this prison and be free. Let me out—I'll pound on the doors till my arms ache and still you don't hear me. Let me out! Let me out! Let me out!

Adult: How can I be with you on this? How can I help you?

Child: Slow down.
         Stop doing all the time.
         Pet simi more
         light candles
         dance
         play games
         don't take everything so seriously
         Hold me
         let me sit on your lap more.
         have tantrums
         cry
         cry
         cry
         cry
         cry

cry I need to cry.
please let me cry.

(In reading back over this dialogue I realize I kept a distance from my Inner Child. I did not connect with her. I did not engage her. I did not "hold her hand.")

DRAWING OUT THE FEELINGS

MATERIALS: Paper, crayons, and felt pens.

When strong emotions come up in your everyday life, let your Inner Child draw them out with your non-dominant hand. Let the drawing be very loose and expressive. You can doodle, scribble, make shapes of color, abstract lines, and forms. If images appear in this spontaneous art, let them emerge. But do not plan the end product. Instead, focus on the *process*, the act of letting feelings come out on paper. Pay special attention to colors, for they express feelings with great accuracy. We're all familiar with common phrases like: "I feel blue" or "He was in a purple rage," or "She saw red," or "I was green with envy." Select the colors spontaneously, using your intuition. Let your Inner Child guide you to the color that best expresses that particular emotion.

AWARENESS

With your dominant hand, write down any observations, feelings, or thoughts about what you have read in this chapter. If you did any or all of the exercises, write a brief summary of your process. What did you learn? What observations, insights, discoveries did you make? This will help you develop the awareness that opens up more choice in your life.

THREE

Embracing Your Vulnerable Child

We enter the world as vulnerable infants—helpless and utterly dependent on adults for getting all of our needs met. We need to be nurtured, protected, and loved—emotionally and physically. And even though we grow in size, that sensitive and fragile little being never disappears. Usually hidden, it lives on and waits for us to reclaim it. I call this highly sensitive and fragile aspect of the Child Within the "Vulnerable Child." This term comes from Voice Dialogue and best describes this aspect of the Inner Child.

It is important to understand that *the Vulnerable Child is only one of many aspects of the Inner Child.* We will meet other aspects—Angry, Playful, Creative, and Spiritual—in later chapters. However, in this chapter we will focus on the Vulnerable Child Within.

What are the characteristics of the Vulnerable Child? It is extremely sensitive to the environment. It feels the energy of others. It tunes into their real selves, especially their unexpressed thoughts and feelings. It picks up body language and attitudes underneath the words. It knows who is telling the truth and who is covering up. Unfortunately, we are taught to deny this fine-tuned radar that our Vulnerable Child has by its very nature. As we learn to listen to it again, that radar can become an incredibly powerful device for navigating through many difficult situations.

How can we tell that the Vulnerable Child is speaking to us? It is simple. We FEEL vulnerable. We may feel fragile and sensitive, in need of nurturing and protection. One way the Vulnerable Child expresses is through physical symptoms such as fatigue, aches, pains, and illness. These are times when we need tender, loving care, just the way a little child does when it feels sick. The same applies when we have been in an accident or sustained some kind of bodily injury. The Vulnerable Child is very evident then.

The Vulnerable Child often comes out through expressions of sorrow, grief, or fear. Tears are a sign of the Vulnerable Child. A strong impulse to hide, to be sheltered, can also be a signal from the Vulnerable Child Within crying, "Protect me! I'm scared. Don't leave me."

When an individual is depressed, that may be an Inner Child who feels beaten down and is therefore extremely vulnerable. Often when a person's Critical Parent Within has been running the show and being abusive, the Inner Child's natural, healthy reaction of anger gets stifled and turns inward. This kills the Child's aliveness and leaves its energy depleted—emotionally and physically. When an adult feels no joy in living that is a sure sign that the Inner Child is locked away. This is not to say that we are supposed to be "happy" all the time. But the Inner Child must be able to feel its feelings, whatever they are. *To rob it of its feelings is to take away its life and its joy.*

Feelings have energy. We may block awareness of our true feelings, but the emotional energy does not go away. It just hides underground and may show up in physical pain, negative moods, obsessive-compulsive behavior, addictions of all kinds, emotional problems, or mental illness. In written conversations the Vulnerable Child will often talk about how and why energy is being blocked. In a therapy session Marilyn's Vulnerable Child said this about her Critical Parent self:

Marilyn's sick all the time because I'm worn out. I've been trying to get her attention for years. I'm tired. She hates her job. I hate her job. But she just doesn't listen to me. The only way I can get her to *not* go to that stupid job is to get sick so she CAN'T go.

Another area of great concern to the Inner Child is personal relationships. This is clearly seen in Sherry's dialogue, in which she discovered what happens when she does not include the Child's needs in her intimate relationship. Her Vulnerable Child wrote:

I never would have married him (ex-husband). If she had asked me what I wanted I would have said, "No, don't do it." I never trusted him. I knew he was dishonest in business and that he'd cheat on her with other women. But she didn't want to listen to my feelings. She was too busy having a good time, at first. But later I really got hurt. Next time she gets into a relationship, I want her to ask me how I feel about the guy.

This plea from the Vulnerable Child highlights how important it is for us to hear its feelings about the people in our lives. That fine-tuned radar of which I spoke earlier is a great gift. If the Vulnerable Child does not feel safe in our so-called intimate relationships, they can never be truly healthy and loving ones. Without safety there can be no trust. Without trust, love flies out the window and leaves fear, anger, or resentment in its place. No one wants to have to wear a suit of armor in his or her own home. That is what happens when we cannot trust the one we are with. We begin to hide for fear of being hurt.

The Vulnerable Child needs to feel safe enough to come out—first with us and then with others who treat it with care. Often in a therapy session or in an Inner Child workshop, a person's Vulnerable Child will begin by talking in a very tentative voice. It is not sure how safe it is to come out. Will it be criticized? There is no way to know for sure. Sometimes it won't talk at first. That is why drawing is so valuable. Many Vulnerable Children who were unwilling to write were able to draw a picture of themselves. That is a wonderful first step. Sometimes the Child will go on to write about the feelings shown in the drawing.

The following drawing speaks for the Vulnerable Child far better than any discourse on the subject could ever do:

this is how i feel sometimes— like i have no skin + no way to keep from being hurt and vulnerable · it hurts physically to be so open +

After making this drawing, Christina wrote a dialogue that helped bring out the pain and frustration of her Vulnerable Child. In this dialogue her child wrote with the non-dominant hand and her adult with the dominant hand.

Child: this is how i feel sometimes—like i have no skin & no way to keep from being hurt and vulnerable. it hurts physically to be so open & yet there's a lot of me i can't let out or let show because it's too painful and scary.

Adult: What do you feel you can't show?

Child: feelings, emotion—like when i try to sing with emotion all i can do is cry. and if i play music from my heart i cry. if i am in front of other people i have to shut down a lot in order to perform & be normal. if i paint realistically i am good at it but it bores me now. if i paint abstract i feel unqualified

& like the art i'm doing is not very good. i also feel held back—i know there's a lot more to let out but i don't know how. i want to paint messy & free but if i do i usually feel like what i do is worth about 10c & it's meaningless to anyone else.

When you do the next exercise be sure you are in a quiet, comfortable, and safe setting. By safe, I mean a place where you can be alone with yourself, with no interruptions or interactions with others. This is quality "alone time" with your Inner Child. If there are abrasive people around or you are in an unsettling atmosphere, your sensitive Vulnerable Child will not want to come out. And rightly so. It is not in this child's best interest to come out around people or situations that are harsh or unresponsive to its needs.

EMBRACING YOUR VULNERABLE CHILD

MATERIALS: Crayons, felt pens, and paper.

1. In your mind's eye picture a very special place where you and your Vulnerable Child can spend some time together. Be sure it is a place where your Inner Child feels safe and comfortable. Take time and visualize any details of the setting. Close your eyes so that you can really "see" this place.

2. With your non-dominant hand, draw a picture of your Vulnerable Child.

3. After your picture is complete, ask your Inner Child if it is okay to talk for a while. Then write out your conversation using both hands as you did in Chapter 2. Ask the Child how it feels. Find out if there are any people or situations that make your Vulnerable Child feel scared, sad, hurt, lonely, etc. Ask the Child what it needs from you, and what you can do to help it feel better.

In this drawing/dialogue, the Child tells about the feelings portrayed in the picture. By asking the Vulnerable Child to put its feelings into its own words, you are gaining insight and understanding. If the Child's response is unclear to you, ask it to explain so you can understand.

Adult: Who are you?

Child: I am you/me. I am a boy/girl - girl boy. My name is Geri. I am quiet & puzzled. There is a lot going on behind my eyes.

Adult: What is that that is going on behind your eyes?

Child: I am hurt and sad. I feel left out. But I don't want to be in because I'm afraid I would shut down or go crazy because I don't understand all this commotion. I am push/pull. I want to and I am afraid to. I am not strong enough but to be swept away.

Adult: Boundary problems. What do you need?

Child: I need space and lots of nonpressured invitations to come in.

Adult: How can I arrange that?

Child: I don't know. Search for comrades. You are doing better than when you were so wrapped up in your adult problems.

This woman drew a picture of her Vulnerable Child that showed different moods. On the right she is crying and clinging to a wall. But on the left she shows the Child being embraced by a warm, loving woman. As we see in her dialogue, she establishes a trusting relationship with her Vulnerable Child.

Adult: When I first saw you, you were pretty terrible looking and cling-ing to the wall, terrible and alone. What's the matter?

Child: I am scared and starving for love and affection. I feel so alone it hurts very badly. I'm not sure of you so I'm watching you shyly to see what youre going to do.

Adult: What would you like me to do?

Child: I want you to stay where you are for awhile and don't move. Just be quiet.

Adult: Okay.

Child: I want to touch you. and look at you. Can I sit on your lap?

Adult: Yes.

Child: Will you stroke my hair? Thank you.

Adult: Why are you so sad? What happened?

Child: I got lost. I got lonely. No one loves me.

Adult: I love you.

Child: You don't act like it.

Adult: I'm sorry. How do you want me to act?

Child: I want you to be nice to me.

Adult: How?

Child: Don't say mean things anymore.

Adult: What else?

Child: Have fun with me. Laugh and hug me and say I love you, you're my precios. And hug me some more. Feed me and brush my hair and clean me up. Wash my face and take me out into the sunshine and play. But mostly stop saying mean things because when you do I want to die and I'm too young to die yet.

Adult: Okay. Do you feel safe yet?

Child: I'm starting to.

Adult: What do you want to do now?

Child: Just sit with you. In your lap.

Sometimes the dialogue can be as simple as asking the Vulnerable Child what it likes, as we see in the next example.

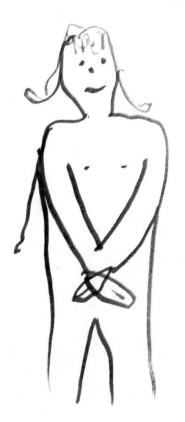

Adult: What do you like?

Child: I like blankies, and silk by my face and chocolate and ice cream and be safe. I like to smell orange blossoms and comfortable clothes. I don't want you to be mad at me when I'm scared. I want you to take care of me. Don't let me eat to much candy. I want you to be in charge and be there for me and it will be okay and tell me I can do it. I don't want to be so serious. Laughing.

LETTING YOUR VULNERABLE CHILD SPEAK

From time to time repeat the previous exercise, "Embracing Your Vulnerable Child." Focus on a different feeling each time. It is advisable to work with feelings that are coming up in your life now. For instance, if a current situation triggers feelings of being abandoned, do this exercise. With your non-dominant hand draw a picture of your Inner Child in this situation. Then continue the exercise doing a right/left-hand dialogue. Here is a list of feelings you can explore with your Vulnerable Child:

Fear
Sadness
Disappointment
Grief
Loneliness
Hurt (emotional or physical)
Abandonment
Sickness
Abuse
Overwhelm
Exhaustion
Despondency
Hopelessness

If the Vulnerable Child has been ignored and abandoned, sometimes when we begin dialoguing it will be angry. Who would not be mad about being left out, being neglected year in and year out? This may happen when you are doing the Inner Child dialogue. The Child may sass back, assert itself, express bottled-up rage and resentment. One never knows if or when this will happen. Just be aware that it is a possibility.

In the following drawing and dialogue by Penny, we see the emergence of an angry child hiding under a vulnerable one. The image in her drawing is unmistakably the Vulnerable Child. Penny even labeled the picture "Heart Hurt." In the dialogue, however, we see the expression of anger from this little Inner Child who says she feels like an "orphan" who "never had a mom or dad." She also talks about being "shellshocked" and "not connected to the heart." Later on in the dialogue when Penny's adult self gets impatient and angry, the Child voice asserts itself, answers back, and demands respect. That is a healthy sign. When the Child expresses anger we know it is safe enough for it to come out and let its true feelings be known. When the downtrodden part of the self speaks up at last, we know we are making progress. In the next chapter there will be opportunities to voice the Angry Child Within. Until then, just be aware that anger can come out when we think we are going to speak to a Vulnerable Child.

Adult: Child, can you tell me your name or something about yourself?

Child: Can't you see by looking at me? I'm not like Big Penny. My hair is a wreck. My clothes are shit. I'm an orphan. I never had a mom or dad. I look like I don't have much hope, shellshocked. I'm not connected to the heart. I'm isolated and unconnected. My posture is stiff and my first image was one hiding behind a heart too afraid to let you see all of me. Definitely I have the ragamuffin look.

Adult: What do you like?

Child: Quilts, places where I can get cozy, be down and be comfortable. Get rid of that hideous pose. I'm tired too. I need some goof-off days. Not shopping. I like to meditate.

Adult: How will I recognize you when you are around?

Child: I demand or want your full attention. No distractions. That is why acupressure is a good thing for you because you stay focused. When you jump all around you are discheveled like this picture. When your head is clear and you're prepared for me is when I'm around.

Adult: What do you dislike?

Child: The steam shovel is my enemy. When people criticize me and I go back inside and get very postured and defensive.

Adult: What keeps you hiding behind that heart? Why don't you come out?

Child: Remember Maslow? Because if I get squelched I stay. There just isn't enough safety. Then there is the mother doormat energy that does the same thing too.

Adult: What are you like? Who are you and what the fuck is your name?

Child: See, you get angry at me. Pump all those questions at me and expect an answer you shit head. Try again - have a little respect.

Adult: So maybe I've expected too much of you?

Child: Not only expected but run steam roller over me. Don't you see?

Adult: Yes I see. Let's go back to what's your name?

Child: Why is that important?

Adult: How will I know you're around?

Child: Softness and gracefulness and graciousness a sense of not being hurried. No time stuff. No agendas. No goals.

A wonderful example of a right/left-hand dialogue in which the Inner Child is allowed to express its feelings is the following one by Tom, who attended one of my workshops.

Adult: Who or what are you?

Child: I am you

Adult: What are you feeling?

Child: I am sad

Adult: Who or what are you?

Child: I am you

Adult: What part of me?

Child: Your sadness

Adult: What to you need right now?

Child: I need to be sad

Adult: Why do you need to be sad right now?

Child: Because nothing has ever gone my way

Adult: Nothing?

Child: That's right—nothing

Adult: What do you want?

Child: I want to be rich, live in a nice house, drive a new car and live happily ever after

Adult: What does happily ever after look like?

Child: It looks fun, and play and no worries and stuff like that.

Adult: That sounds great to me—How do we get it?

Child: I don't know—

Adult: You are a pretty creative guy—How about some ideas.

Child: I don't know—I'm afraid

Adult: What are you afraid of

Child: Everything—I'm just a kid—what do I know.

Adult: How old are you?

Child: 4

James reported to me that the following dialogue had been a powerful breakthrough experience for him. As he contacted his Inner Child by writing with this non-dominant hand, he twice broke down and cried. For the first time in his life, he felt a deep conscious connection with his Inner Child, especially the vulnerable aspect.

Writing with my left hand feels a bit akward, but if it will help me to become more complete and to help release the frightened child within to come out and play I'll sit here all day and write.

I miss playing. I would like more fun in my life. I love you. I'm sorry we didn't do this before. I can feel the fear in the child that is hiding in the shadows of my mind. All I wanted was love, my mommy and Daddy to love me. There was so much pain when they fought. Why did they become mean to each other? Whey did they take their love away from me and my brothers? I had to run and hide. I was feeling too much pain and loneliness. No one was paying any attention to me. Please help me. I need love, I want to come out and play. I want to laugh and sing! I want to play play play! And to feel loved!

After his Inner Child wrote, he continued with a longer, more detailed response describing his experience:

> As I wrote more with my left hand, I began to feel like a child. I started to release some deep emotional feelings—ones I may have shared very lightly with people who I trusted. As the child in me started to emerge, I began to feel mistrust and where I was at emotionally as a child when this mistrust began. I felt lost, alone, and full of fear. I admire the child for finally coming out and taking the risk of telling me how he was really feeling. We both were so afraid to tell each other how we felt. It was difficult to look at the issues and feel the pain, but it has to come out. I don't want to feel suppressed any longer. I want love and joy in my life.

Illness and the Inner Child

One of the most obvious ways that the Inner Child expresses is through sickness. When you are ill or in physical pain your Vulnerable Child is speaking. It needs tenderness, love, and understanding. This is a time to nurture yourself. Nurturing begins when we listen to the feelings and needs of that little Child inside. Accepting it when it is not feeling well is a wonderful way to honor the Inner Child. Instead of telling it to get to work or berating it for being sickly and weak, you can pay attention to its needs. You may even ask for help from others so that you can focus on caring for the Child Within. As you do this, you will be strengthening your Nurturing Parent (as we shall see in a later chapter). This reassures the Child that it will not be abandoned or forced to act well when it does not *feel* well.

One of the best ways to truly hear what that Vulnerable Child is saying is to talk with your body. Yes, you read correctly: I did say TALK with your body. Have a little heart-to-heart chat with the part of your body that hurts. Your Inner Child is in there and has something to say.

One of my readers had a powerful experience dialoguing with the body. Sue, an American artist living with her husband in Japan, had found a version of this dialogue technique in my book, *The Well-Being Journal.* In a letter, she wrote:

> The exercise . . . precipitated a real breakthrough for me in healing the Inner Child. I felt tension in the area around my neck, mouth, head, etc., as usual, and as I was laying there I had the definite impression that it was because I had something to say that I had needed to verbalize very badly for a long time. Boy was that ever right. I also had a dream that reinforced my feeling about this. And as a result I was able to say out loud for the first time in my life the things I had wanted to say, as a child, to my alcoholic mother and my overbearing stepfather. It was quite a session I had, and also made me realize that we have as much need to say and physically do these healing exercises as we have to write about them. The writing opened up for me the ability to then say and do.

Sue also shared some profound insights about the relationship between her wounded Inner Child and her physical condition. She wrote that in working with the Inner Child she learned to identify areas that needed healing in her life. This made her realize:

> that my journey in healing this past four years has been the last part of unraveling the problem of being a child of an alcoholic. The neck problem developed as a result of years of "hanging my head in shame"— which caused an actual physical problem that needed help from a chiropractor. But the inner healing that I have been doing, which has

also helped heal the neck problem, is the even bigger issue. I am so grateful that it all happened so that I could have this chance to grow more and change and unravel lots of problems that I couldn't resolve in the past.

In the next exercise, you will use the drawing and dialoguing technique presented earlier. This time, you will be picturing your body and dialoguing with any part of it that is in stress or pain. These are the places through which your Vulnerable Child is trying to speak to you.

I might add that this is an excellent exercise to do on a regular basis as a way of preventing problems. When you do this body dialogue, you are really tuning into your Inner Child's physical and emotional needs. It is advisable to do this exercise at the first sign of any symptoms of illness. My own personal experiences and those of my students, clients, and readers tells me that this ounce of prevention is definitely worth a pound of cure.

TALKING WITH MY BODY

MATERIALS: Paper and felt pens.

1. Sit quietly and tune in to your body. Check to see if there are any areas that are tense, sore, or painful. If there are more than one, just make a mental note of it. Now select one body part and really feel the sensations there.

2. With your non-dominant hand draw a picture of this body part, using colors that express the sensations there.

3. Now do a dialogue in which you interview the body part. Write the questions with your dominant hand. Let your body part answer with your non-dominant hand. Use two different colored pens. Let the body part speak with one of the colors in your drawing. In your interview ask the body part to tell you its name, i.e., lungs, left leg, etc. Then ask it how it feels and why it feels that way. Finally, ask the body part what you can do to make it feel better.

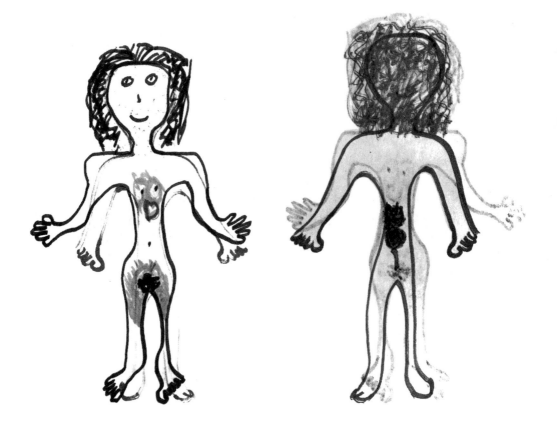

Me: Who or what are you?

Body: I ur kid nee beans & low back & I sore.

Me: How do you feel?

Body: Tight & mad—no I good n mad. I keep it all here in a tight ball—haf to put it somewhur—so I put it all here.

Me: Why do you feel that way?

Body: U hold in n hold back u hold in yur back—think people don't see don't kno—u keep a good front—but tie up ur back—carry everything der. it 2 much 4 me—don't want NO MORE! ENUFF!

Me: What can I do to help you?

Body: Feel things in right places—let dem do some of de wurk—let yur other parts help to. Use all of yurself. Then I won't get so tired.

MOVING WITH FEELING

MATERIALS: Recorded music and sound system.

1. Find some recorded music that expresses the feelings of your Vulnerable Child: sadness, loneliness, fear, etc.

2. Play the music and as you listen let your body move into postures or gestures that express that particular feeling. Let your Inner Child move the feelings out spontaneously. Do not worry about how you look. No one is watching except you. There is no right or wrong way, only your Inner Child's dance. You may find that your Inner Child wants props, i.e., a stuffed animal, a blanket; or it may want to be in the corner or some cozy, safe place.

The Vulnerable Child and Survival Needs

Another way the Vulnerable Child shows up is in our survival issues. If we have beliefs that we are not competent enough to support ourselves, the Inner Child will be in a perpetual state of anxiety. Think about a little child being raised by parents who cannot adequately feed, clothe, or house it. There is the constant fear that there will not be enough. In fact, there are many fairy tales based on this theme. "Hansel and Gretel" and "The Little Match Girl" are among the many stories that tell about children whose parents were too poor to take care of them. If we do not have a strong Nurturing Parent as well as a Protective Parent Within who can deal effectively with the outer world, that Inner Child will be in a constant state of fear. Survival is a basic issue. We all must deal with it. If we haven't handled that area of our lives, we are on very shaky ground.

Much of my private client work has included career counseling. This theme of the poverty-stricken child or the hungry waif has recurred again and again. In written dialogues and in therapy sessions, the Vulnerable Child expresses its fears that it will not be taken care of materially. This fear exists for rich and poor alike. It has little to do with the person's material circumstances. He or she may be doing quite well or may be struggling to make ends meet. But the little waif is still living inside, anxious about where the next meal is coming from or if it will have a roof over its head tomorrow or the next day or the next. Sometimes the fear comes from actual experiences of poverty in childhood. Even though the present reality is quite different, the memories of deprivation linger on in the Inner Child. This can even lead to severe workaholism, as the adult self attempts to run away from poverty. But again, the Inner Child is left behind. There is no room in a workaholic's life for the Child Within, least of all the Vulnerable Child.

This condition of deep-seated anxiety about survival may also be the result of having parents who went through the Great Depression and never forgot or got over it. No matter how affluent these Depression survivors became later, the idea of losing everything haunts many of them like a silent terror. They "teach" it to their children. It is almost as if those old fears are transferred genetically to the next generation. The same is true for children of survivors of the World War II holocaust. And, of course, those of us who are clinicians see survivors of more recent holocausts: Vietnam veterans, and immigrants from war-torn countries all over the globe.

AWARENESS

MATERIALS: Paper and pen.

With your dominant hand, write out any insights you have gained about your Vulnerable Child. If you did the exercises, summarize what happened. Be an observer, recording what you saw and heard without judgment. By learning to watch and listen with an open mind, you can develop a deeper level of awareness about your self.

FOUR
Accepting Your Angry Child

It is popular these days to focus on the "precious child," or "the magical child," or the "divine child." I certainly support getting to know all these aspects, and we will meet them later on in the book. However, I see the Inner Child as very human, containing light and dark sides, pleasant and not so pleasant faces. In my work I am concerned with the whole child, not just the pretty, neat, and cute parts. So I will be exploring the less popular aspects of the Inner Child. We've already met one of them, the Vulnerable Child. But perhaps the least understood and most feared aspect is the Angry Child.

In the literature on Inner Child healing one does not hear much about the Angry Child. It is as if the Angry Child Within were the "black sheep" of the Inner Family. I have not heard of any model of therapy that actually identifies this sub-personality. But I have certainly experienced it in myself and others. I feel the Angry Child deserves its place along with all the other "more acceptable" kids, so I've dedicated this chapter to it. I've also included a section on the selfish Inner Brat, perhaps the most disowned aspect of the Inner Child.

Anger is a natural reaction to mistreatment. Anger can be an important survival tool. When a child has been mistreated, criticized, shamed, punished, or ostracized, it is natural for it to feel some anger. But if anger is taboo, then insult is added to injury. When we were children, lots of things happened to us that made us mad. If we were not allowed to express our anger in safe ways, if anger was forbidden or considered dangerous, then our Angry Child probably went underground.

Sometimes people who have difficulty feeling and expressing anger are terrified because they are afraid they might erupt like a volcano. That is understandable. When anger gets buried year in and year out, it is like a land mine that could go off at any time. These individuals fear violence, often because they were raised in a violent household, with parents who exploded like time bombs for no apparent reason. Anger became associated with confusion and chaos. Sometimes it was connected with alcoholism, because the parent's rage and violence burst through in drunkenness.

Anger that goes underground often hides out in the body: headaches, high blood pressure, heart disease, cancer, and other conditions have been associated with anger that is held in. Unexpressed anger is also an aspect of the co-dependency pattern, in which hurtful treatment from others is glossed over, rationalized, or totally denied. Scribbling our anger out the way a young child does can go a long way toward helping us accept and release these difficult feelings.

DRAWING YOUR ANGER OUT

MATERIALS: Several sheets of plain newsprint 18″ x 24″ and crayons (preferably fat kindergarten crayons).

1. Think of the last time you felt really angry. Remember the situation and how you felt inside. Now ask your Inner Child to do some

angry scribbles with your non-dominant hand. Choose colors that express anger. Do as many of these angry drawings as you wish.

2. Let your Angry Child actually draw a picture of itself (with your non-dominant hand). Give the picture a title.

Talking with Your Angry Child

Many people have great difficulty responding to the needs of their Inner Child. If our own parents did not set a good example, we had no models for healthy parenting. Therefore, we do not know how to take care of our Inner Child. The Child Within feels abandoned and angry because it has had to fend for itself with no guidance and with no love or nurturing. It wants to be cared for, but when it looks for an Inner Parent, nobody's home.

There is hope, however. Through dialoguing we can open lines of communication and cultivate a healthy parent-child relationship within. As the Child feels safer, it will take risks and begin to express the anger it has been harboring for so long. The Child may even start making demands. As uncomfortable as it seems, this is usually a sign of progress. The Child simply will not be intimidated any longer and is speaking up. This is a time to be quiet long enough to hear the Child's feelings and needs. The next exercise is entitled "Good and Mad." Many of the examples that follow show the Child asserting itself. Sometimes a dialogue with a newly emerging Angry Child will seem to end in a stalemate. The important thing is to keep communicating through drawing and written dialogues.

GOOD AND MAD

MATERIALS: Paper, crayon, and felt pens.

1. Have a written conversation with your Angry Child. With your dominant hand, ask the child to tell you about what it's like to feel mad. What makes it mad? Let the Angry Child respond with your non-dominant hand. Let it tell you what it would like to do when it gets angry. How does it want you, the adult, to let it feel and express anger in your everyday life?

2. Next time you feel angry sit down and have a talk with your Angry Child. You (the adult) write with the dominant hand; your Angry Child writes with the non-dominant hand.

i am mad   i hate this
i thought
i could
speak
once
+ be
done
with it
i hate
having to   talk.

Adult: Hi.

Child: Hi.

Adult: What do you want to tell me?

Child: I'm here

Adult: I want to know you.

Child: Fuck off

Adult: Why are you so angry?

Child: Nobody took care of me.

Adult: Is that really it?

Child: I felt like that

Adult: Why don't you have hands or feet?

Child: I don't know.

Adult: I don't like you.

Child: I don't like you either

Adult: Let's be friends. OK?

Child: OK.

Adult: I'm sorry I hurt your feelings. I thought I already knew who you were.

Child: I know but you don't. All that stuff is childhood memories.

Adult: Who are you? then really?

Child: The inner child not your childhood child

Adult: Oh. That's a big difference.

Child: You think you know me but you haven't even met me.

Adult: Ho. I'm beginning to get it. I want to know more please.

Child: Sigh. Thanks for finding—you have to look—keep looking til you can really tell its me

Adult: Good—thanks—Do you want to talk some more now?

Child: I love you.

Adult: I feel myself getting side tracked—are you still there?—Do you feel safe to talk?

Child: Not here—not now

Adult: OK

When people draw and dialogue, the Child may sometimes begin by expressing happiness and playful feelings, perhaps sadness. But then the anger comes out. This may be triggered by a critical or uncaring comment from the "adult" voice (dominant hand). An excellent example of this is seen in the following drawing and dialogue by Susan:

Hi! I'm Suzie. I'm Happy - I like my smile - I can Run And I like To play But Sometimes I'm Sad

The following is Susan's dialogue with her Inner Child:

Child: Hi! I'm Suzie. I'm happy—I like my smile. I can run and I like to play but sometimes I'm sad.

Adult: Why are you sad Suzie?

Child: I'm sad because mommy and daddy don't want to play.

Adult: What are they doing?

Child: They're working. They don't have time to play. Please play with me. I feel so sad.

Adult: Come Suzie. Lets go play.

Child: Can we play by the flowers.

Adult: Yes we can go anywhere you like. Where would you like to go?

Child: I want to go in the pasture. Can we go there?

Adult: Yes. Can you show me the way?

Child: I like you. Can you stay for a while.

Adult: I can stay as long as you like.

Child: I'm happy. I feel cozy. Will you take care of me?

Adult: You'll have to learn to take care of yourself.

Child: You're bad!! Really BAD BAD BAD

Adult: Now you don't like me!?

Child: You're mean.

Adult: I feel mean and part of me pushes you away. I could have said I'll help take care of you and I'll help you learn to take care of yourself. You're right. I am mean sometimes even though I love you. That's alot to say to a little girl. What are you thinking.

Child: It's not fair. You're too mean. You should tak care of me.

Adult: I think I haven't grown up enough and even now I'm not feeling truthfully compassionate to say those things I know I should—I'm not a very good adult.

Child: So who's going to take care of me. I'm feeling abandoned. Who's going to show me how.

Adult: And I wonder why I am withholding from you. Nobody helped me grow up.

Child: But you should know better.

Adult: Not really. I'm sad too.

Child: Why can't you let me cry. Why do you always make me feel bad. Do I always have to take care of you.

Adult: I guess I'm a spoiled child.

Child: Why can't you grow up!

Adult: It seems like I'm always taking all the attention—you feel like there's none left over for you.

Child: That's right and I'm mad and I'm going to make you unhappy.

Adult: And how are you going to do that.

Child: I'm going to cry all the time and then you can't be happy either—so there!

Adult: This sounds pretty serious.

Child: Yes—all the time you're serious and we never get to play.

Adult: I'm really disturbed about this.

Child: You should be.

Adult: And now you're trying to make me feel guilty.

Child: This sounds like a stand off.

As we develop communication with our Inner Child, the Child's voice gets stronger. It will begin asserting itself against negligence, manipulation, or harsh self-criticism. The Child will demand nurturance and protection.

As uncomfortable as it seems, this is usually a sign of progress. If a standoff occurs, as it did in the previous example, be patient. Give the process some time. Your Inner Parent may need to mature and to change its attitude toward the Child. It is sometimes hard for adults to admit they were wrong. Resume dialoguing later and see what develops. You may be surprised. Also, remember that there are some chapters ahead in which you will learn to develop a strong Nurturing and Protective Inner Parent.

Some dialogues yield profound insights about the psychological damage done to a child who is not allowed to express his or her anger in healthy ways. Anger becomes associated with evil and must be hidden at all costs. Furthermore, the child who feels angry concludes that he or she is bad for even having such feelings. This puts an abused child in a double bind. It is natural and normal to feel anger toward parents who abuse us. But if we are punished for feeling angry, the anger just gets pushed deeper and deeper inside.

In the next dialogue, Sue's Angry Child vents her rage about childhood abuse which went unexpressed for years. The most significant part of her dialogue is the line written by her Inner Child, "I am bad I want to kill you [her abusive parents] I must kill myself & not want to feel my anger. . . . I feel frozen inside. . . . like a dead girl . . . I have killed myself dead. . . . I am lost in my numbness of no feeling please come and rescue me. . . ." When we kill our feelings we kill our Inner Child. When we kill our Inner Child we kill our true Selves.

Is it anger or something sinister. It is something very basic. Something black a shadow which has a white side too. Why why why —

Of what in myself am I afraid. What savage beast? Is it anger? I have certainly begun to express that.

Adult: What is needing to be out? What am I repressing? Is it the need to give—the need to love, the need to care, the need to serve? I don't know. I will trust this to my healer—that it will appear at the right time. Is it anger or something sinister? Is it something very basic. Something black as a shadow which has a white side too. Why why why—of what in myself am I afraid? What savage beast? Is it anger? I have certainly begun to express that. Does my playful child have a destructive side that needs to be expressed in a childful way?

Child: No good mommy. daddy always fighting. I hate you always yelling and fighting and mean. Bad bad mommy and daddy—die die die. go away & stay away so I won't kill you you are so mean and cruel & you dont love Susie anymore mean mommy & daddy. HATE HATE KILL KILL. Love love me we. I am bad I want to kill you I must kill myself & not want to feel my anger my love I am bad bad girl I try to kill my mommy and my daddy. I am so so angry at mommy & daddy. I feel frozen inside. Like a dead girl a dead man—I have killed myself dead—where am I I dont know I want feel myself anymore I am lost in my numbness of no feeling please come and rescue me and help me feel again that is what you can do for me—make my child self feel again and experience the beautiful world—color, music, birds, song, love, peace, joy.

Anger is an active emotion. Its expression is clearly outward. When people are angry they often make loud sounds, broad gestures, and even violent movements. A wonderful medium for releasing anger without hurting others or the environment is ceramic clay. This malleable, earthy substance is perfect for active movements. With it you can hit, throw, punch, pound, twist, poke, or chop safely without damaging it or yourself.

It is true that pillows and cushions can be used for expressing anger. However, in my art therapy practice I have observed that clay is far more satisfying for clients who need to vent anger or rage. What is unique about clay is that after "beating it up" and taking out all your feelings on it, you can reshape and reuse it immediately. When the anger has been released and new feelings arise, the clay can reflect the shift in mood. Clay is neutral. It becomes whatever you are. It expresses whatever you feel at the moment.

ANGRY CLAY PLAY

MATERIALS: Wet ceramic clay and hard work surface (masonite, plastic, or wood, etc.).

1. Let your Angry Child express itself with clay. Allow it to pound and hit and flatten the clay, using your fist or the flat of your hand. Forget about making a finished product, just let your angry kid come out and play with the clay.

2. The next time you get really mad about something, make time and space to express your anger with clay.

3. If you don't have any clay available, try punching some pillows or cushions. Padded bats called battacas are also available for venting anger. They are used in therapeutic settings as a safe method for releasing rage.

NOTE:

Wet ceramic clay is available in art stores in 25-pound bags. The clay must be kept airtight in a sealed plastic bag or refrigerator container with lid. Otherwise it will dry up, harden, and be unusable.

One way we can often tell how others feel is by watching the changes on their faces. Research has been done on emotional expression as it affects the facial muscles. In fact, certain feelings that become chronic can freeze themselves into a person's face and become part of his or her habitual facial expression. For instance, some people wear worry or anger on their faces in permanent frown lines between their eyebrows. These deep furrows are engraved over time, like riverbeds that form in a landscape over thousands of years. Instead of holding anger in and etching those frown lines onto your face, you can let those feelings out through art. It can be great fun.

Many years ago I had a very powerful experience drawing my anger out. I had been treated dishonestly by someone I considered a good friend. My Angry Child was boiling. This was extremely frustrating because I could not locate the person in order to express my feelings. I also had no time because I had to conduct a weekly class in Art for Teachers of Young Children at a local college. What to do? As I was leaving home to teach the class, I remembered that it was Kid's Night (a monthly event in which the students actually brought children in for arts activities). I ran into my studio and got mask-making supplies so that I could participate in the workshop and get my pent-up feelings out. During one segment of the evening, I joined a group of little artists and made a wonderful monster mask with green skin, purple hair, red eyes, and a long, red tongue sticking out of a mouth with jagged teeth. The kids loved it. It seemed to give them permission to make their own angry masks. We all had great fun wearing our masks, growling and laughing at each other.

MAD MASK

MATERIALS: Grocery bag large enough to slip over your head, crayons, felt pens, and scissors.

1. Make a mask out of an inverted grocery bag by cutting out holes for the eyes and mouth. Let your angry Inner Child draw its face on the mask. Let the face really show anger through color and facial expression, i.e., teeth showing, tongue sticking out, frown, etc.

2. Put your mask on and look at yourself in the mirror. Have fun making angry sounds, i.e., growling, etc.

3. Display your angry mask somewhere in the environment as a way of honoring your angry child.

Physical activity is a great way to let off steam: jumping, hopping, skipping, slamming a ball with a racket, or doing spontaneous dance/movement. These are all ways to "move the anger out," to express it, to celebrate it, instead of stuffing it down.

MOVING YOUR ANGER OUT

MATERIALS: Some recorded music that expresses angry energy, i.e., staccato rhythms with drums and other percussion instruments.

1. Play the music and allow your body to move angry feelings out. Be spontaneous, and respond to the rhythm. Avoid clichés and learned "dance steps." This is your Angry Child's dance.

2. Do an Angry Dance with your Mad Mask on. Dance your anger in front of a mirror. If you feel okay about being photographed, ask someone to take a snapshot of you in your mask doing your Angry Dance.

The Inner Brat

Inside all of us there is a selfish brat who wants what it wants WHEN it wants it. This is a self-centered aspect of the Inner Child who believes that the world revolves around its whims and desires. Of course, most of us do not admit to having an Inner Brat, because bratty behavior (in adults and children) is generally considered unacceptable in our society. The only people who get away with it are the rich and famous, and authority figures. For instance, many stars in the entertainment industry are notorious for throwing temper tantrums. As creative artists they are very much in touch with their Inner Child. They *have to* be. Playfulness, emotional sensitivity, and a well-developed imagination—all qualities of the Inner Child—are what give entertainers and artists their creative genius and charisma. That's the good news. The bad news is that when one lives in the Inner Child state much of the time, and gets applauded and rewarded for it with fame and fortune, the Bratty Child is also very accessible.

A classic case of an Inner Brat run rampant is the character Arthur (played by Dudley Moore) in the movie of the same name. Arthur got away with his irreverent, self-indulgent behavior because he was rich and was allowed to do whatever he pleased. His alcoholism was tolerated or overlooked. His obnoxious behavior was permitted to go unchecked simply because he did not have to deal with any consequences.

With the death of his co-dependent personal servant (played by John Gielgud), Arthur finds a replacement in a co-dependent girlfriend (played by Liza Minnelli). As might be expected, she is also the adult child of an alcoholic father, and has had lots of experience playing the role of rescuer. After many trials and tribulations, the movie ends with the couple going off to live "happily ever after."

The film was very popular. Everyone loved Arthur. However, in *Arthur II* reality set in, as it usually does sooner or later. The film was monumentally boring, as only an old drunk can be. What was irreverently funny in the first film became tedious in the second. It was clear that living with an alcoholic, self-indulgent brat is no joke. And the thought of such an individual becoming a parent is positively horrifying.

The story of Arthur is a dramatic example of what happens when a person's Inner Brat is allowed to run his or her life. It can lead to addictions of many kinds and gross abuses of the rights and needs of others. Of course, a brat may be amusing for a short time, because he or she may be acting out the irreverence that many of us feel but are afraid to express. But when an individual is stuck in or identified with the Inner Brat the humor wears thin rather quickly.

As mentioned earlier, most people deny the existence of their Inner Brat. They will let others act it out. Nowhere is this more obvious than in the case of parents who appear to be pillars of society, upstanding citizens, and virtuous members of the church, and yet have adolescent children who are juvenile delinquents. Friends and neighbors are usually incredulous in the face of such family dynamics. The typical reaction is, " How could such *nice* parents have such rotten kids?" It is a good question.

I once taught the parents of adolescents on probation through a local family services agency. These parents were directed by the court system to take classes in effective parenting. Most of the parents who attended were totally identified with their Critical Parent sub-personality. The other parents slept through the class or attended sporadically. The ones who identified with their Critical Parent were extremely controlled individuals who did not express emotion (positive or negative), who had unrealistically high expectations for their children, and who never acknowledged their children for a job well done. Nothing was ever good enough for these parents. They were perfectionists. They would have been the last people in the world to admit that they had a selfish, bratty bone in their bodies. In fact, many of them were heard to say, "After all we've done for this kid, how could he (or she) act this way?" Such parents believed they had sacrificed themselves for their children. And certainly they did give their families a great deal materially. But *emotionally* their children were starving to death. They ended up acting out their parents' disowned Inner Brats. It was the only way they could get attention.

Healing From the Inner Brat

Although the Inner Brat is one of the most disowned aspects of the Inner Child, acknowledging this sub-personality can open up a lot of energy. It takes a great deal of emotional and physical effort to suppress or repress the Inner Brat. Let's face it, there are times when we all want our own way at any cost. That does not mean that we necessarily *act* in such a manner, but if we squelch the *feeling* we do ourselves a disservice. Anyone who has ever been on a busy freeway at rush hour knows what I am talking about. When people are in a hurry or when they are hungry and tired after a long day's work, they can very easily act like two-year-olds. They will push and shove, literally and figuratively, to get their way. That is the Inner Brat.

I am by no means advocating that people allow their Inner Brat free reign, as that would lead to chaos and anarchy. What I have discovered, however, is that if we are unaware of our selfish, bratty impulses, and choose to cover them up or block them off entirely, we run the risk of making ourselves sick. In private practice and in groups for individuals with life-threatening or chronic illness, I have seen dramatic transformations when the Inner Brat is acknowledged.

It is believed by many psychologists that cancer is related to anger turned inward toward the self. In my own clinical experience, I have observed that unleashing the Inner Brat in a safe, productive way can have immense therapeutic value. When I was struggling with that life-threatening disease, and entered psychotherapy, my therapist gave me permission to let my Brat out. She encouraged me to have a temper tantrum by beating up an effigy of the doctors who had misdiagnosed and overmedicated me. By giving me a safe space in which to accept and vent my Inner Brat, she helped me empower myself both psychologically and physically. This process was an important part of my healing without medication.

An anonymous workshop participant captured the essence of the Inner Brat in this monologue written with the non-dominant hand. More important, there was no attempt to make the bratty, Angry Child change or go away. All it wants is to be accepted and heard.

ANGRY CHILD SPEAKS

Let me be obnoxious. Let me be a brat.
Let me sing.
Let me say *NO*. Let me be irresponsible

let me SCREAM
let me yell & hit & be cheered on for it. let me cuddle
Calm me down.
Be nice to me. Be calm & sweet & protective.
& take care of $ & car & don't push me around.
Keep being forgiving
Remind me to breathe
Give me time to shout & sing & turn & jump & dance. Let me
dance &
let me rest.
Find
  Balance
    For
      Me.
Hugs.

AWARENESS

Writing with your dominant hand, jot down any reactions to the material on the Angry Child you have just read. Did you do any of the exercises? If so, look at your work in the order you did it and get an overview of your experience. Write down your observations and insights in as neutral a way as possible. Avoid "solutions" or criticism; just report what happened.

PART II

Exploring Your Inner Parent

We nurture and protect the Child Within by calling forth a part of us called the Inner Parent. This Parent Within learns how to do its job from our own parents or caregivers in childhood. If they were good models of healthy parenting, then we develop a strong and loving Inner Parent. But if we have had inadequate parenting in childhood, we don't know what a healthy parent-child relationship *feels* like. For this reason, people who were raised in dysfunctional families have great difficulty responding to the needs of their Inner Child. The Inner Child of such an adult is often very sad or angry. An Inner Child who has to fend for itself resents not having Inner Parents to help and guide it. When it looks for care and protection, nobody's home. Ultimately the Child is left feeling frightened, sad, angry, lonely, and empty.

The paradox is that many adults whose Inner Child is abandoned *do* have well-developed nurturing and protective abilities. But unfortunately they have turned these abilities *outward toward others*. They nurture and protect everyone but themselves. Their family members, friends, neighbors, employers, coworkers, clients all come first. Their Inner Child comes last.

In childhood, many of these individuals had to be "little parents" to their siblings or to their real parents (who were drunk, ill, or absent). They had to do this in order to survive. But unfortunately, they continue in adulthood to rescue others, when it is no longer necessary for survival. The rewards for being a rescuer are many: approval from others, jobs, money. After all, rescuers are so handy to have around. They are often dependable, hard workers.

Certainly there is nothing wrong with dependability, but when it is used exclusively for the benefit of others, to the detriment of the Inner Child, then something is very wrong. There is an old phrase, "Charity begins at home." What good is it to care for others when one's own Inner Child is locked up at home starving to death? Our task, then, is to find the Nurturing Parent Within, as well as our own Protective Parent.

In earlier chapters you actually began the re-parenting process. Whether you realized it or not, by dialoguing with your Inner Child you were activating a healthy Inner Parent. For instance, asking questions and caring enough to hear the Child's feelings is a way to strengthen the *Nurturing* Parent Within. When you reassure your Child and tell it how much you love it and want to take care of it, your Nurturing Parent is present. It is your Nurturing Parent who soothes your Inner Child with understanding and compassion and who provides it with healthy enjoyment. And when you deal with the outer world in a way that meets your Inner Child's needs, your *Protective* Parent is at work. Setting limits, maintaining boundaries, asserting your Child's rights are all ways that your Protective Parent serves your Inner Child.

In some of the earlier dialogue examples you also heard another parental voice: the Critical Parent. We all have one. It is the perfectionist, the taskmaster who pushes us mercilessly. It shames us and belittles us and wreaks havoc with our self-confidence. Nothing we do is ever good enough for the Critical Parent. It specializes in finding fault.

The next three chapters are devoted to all these aspects of the Inner Parent: *nurturing, protective,* and *critical.* By learning to recognize when they are active, we can choose how to let them express. We can learn to recognize signs that the Critical Parent has taken over. We can also tell if our Nurturing or Protective Parent is serving our own Inner Child or rescuing the Inner Child of others and thereby creating co-dependence. For as I mentioned in Chapter 1, every adult is responsible for his or her own Inner Child's welfare. *Sooner or later, we must become our own parents.*

So let us start by finding the Nurturing Parent Within.

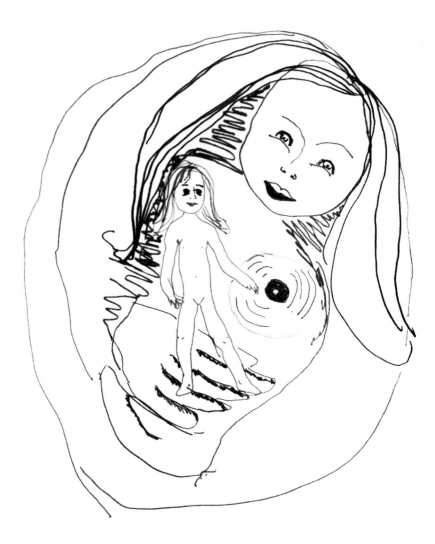

FIVE

Finding the Nurturing Parent Within

Just as the child appears throughout history as a symbol of potential, renewal, and growth, the Nurturing Parent is also a universal archetype. In fact, the oldest examples of art by our earliest ancestors are sculptures of women as Earth Mother. These fertility goddesses were formed out of earth, with large breasts and hips. Some of them have many breasts, as if to say: "I am an inexhaustible source of life and sustenance."

The Nurturing Parent archetype appears in all cultures, usually in the image of a woman. In the Hindu pantheon the goddess Lakshmi is the giver of wealth and abundance. In China, her name is Kuan yin, the bestower of compassion. In the Native American tradition she appears as White Buffalo Woman.

Of course, the most popular version of the Nurturing Parent in European culture is the Blessed Mother or Mary, mother of Jesus. For nearly two thousand years, she has been rendered in every possible medium and style. We see her in Byzantine mosaics, painted wood icons, Gothic windows, Renaissance murals, and marble sculptures. The image of the madonna and child as fashioned by the masters appears in all the great museums. She can also be seen in the humblest of remote country shrines.

As Jung, Campbell, and Neumann have shown, the Great Mother archetype is a reflection of a universal aspect of the human psyche. In honoring the Great Goddess we pay our respects to Nature. To revere Earth Mother is to acknowledge our need for physical sustenance, as well as emotional support. We are her children. This symbol of the Nurturing Parent also embodies qualities like empathy, understanding, compassion, and caring. We all have these qualities within. We can find them and use them in re-parenting ourselves.

As we shall see, this Nurturing Parent is closely connected with our Higher Power or Higher Self. It makes the spirit of divine love manifest on a day-to-day basis. For it is through consistent and intimate care that a Nurturing Parent truly demonstrates love for its infant. Parents show love in all the little thankless tasks they perform: feedings in the middle of the night, changing diapers, caring for the sick child, cleaning up its messes, consoling it when it gets hurt. Later on the parent nurtures by respecting the child's need for autonomy and teaches the child to take care of itself. This takes time and patience, and more love. As the old Chinese proverb tells us: "Give a man a fish and you feed him for a day; teach him how to fish and you feed him for life." Healthy parenting means knowing when to give and when not to give, when to help and when to encourage independence. For the archetype of the Nurturing Parent is about sustenance, abundance, and plentitude. A child who is lovingly guided in how to take care of itself integrates the qualities of the Nurturing Parent into itself. Such a child grows up with a direct connection to all the qualities represented in the Earth Mother Goddesses.

A healthy parent also expresses love when he or she plays with the child. By delighting in just *being together*, the parent shows acceptance for the child just as it is. This is not to say that the parent permits any kind of behavior. Not at all. It simply means that the child is acknowledged as being worthwhile as a child. It is accepted unconditionally as its own unique self, at its particular stage of development (not when it is taller, or older, or smarter).

Countless clients and workshop participants have said that it is the easiest thing in the world to give love and care to others, but that when it comes to nurturing *themselves* it is a different story. In fact, they often describe self-nurturing as *the most difficult task they have ever had to do.*

We grow up being told to be unselfish, to share, to put others first. The golden rule is taught in a distorted form. It admonishes us to *love others as you love yourself.* But the "as you love yourself" part gets overlooked. The paradox is that a person who doesn't care for and nurture him or herself has less to give others: less energy, less enthusiasm, and less love.

It is a well-known fact that focusing all of our nurturing abilities (our Nurturing Parent) toward others, to the detriment of our own self-care, creates co-dependent relationships. Marla is preoccupied with the problems of her drug-addicted boyfriend, Todd. She rescues him at every turn. She loans him money and makes his car payments when he has spent all his money on drugs. When he misses work, he talks her into calling his boss with excuses for his absence. She readily complies.

Marla's Nurturing Parent is off rescuing Todd's Inner Child (who becomes panic-stricken when faced with the consequences of his irresponsible be-havior). She does not want to see his Inner Child hurt. So she tries to help him avoid the consequences of that behavior. But the fact is that Todd, not Marla, is responsible for his Inner Child. In taking over the job of being the Protective and Nurturing Parent to Todd's Inner Child, she neglects her own Inner Child. She feels exhausted and anxious much of the time.

In a dialogue with her Inner Child, Marla hears the truth in no uncertain terms: *"Take care of me!* I'm your own child. Todd is a grown-up. Let him take care of his own kid. You take care of me. I'm sick and tired all the time because nobody is here for me. I'm starving to death. Help me."

With the help of Co-dependents Anonymous or C.O.D.A. (a 12-step pro-gram for co-dependence) and continued dialogues in which she re-parented her Inner Child, Marla broke free from the destructive relationship. When she stopped rescuing her boyfriend, he found another co-dependent woman to "play mother" to his Inner Child. His addiction became worse and he finally ended up bankrupt and abandoned by his drug-using friends. When a desperate Todd contacted Marla once again in hopes of being rescued, she was able to say no. Thanks to the strength she had developed from both her involvement in C.O.D.A. and her re-parenting process, she was able to care for her Inner Child. No longer would she collude with Todd and prolong his unhealthy dependence on her. She was heeding her own Inner Child's plea: Take care of me!

Opening your heart to the needs of your own Inner Child is the true beginning of re-parenting. Finding the Nurturing Parent Within and turning that tender loving care inward on a daily basis is the first step toward healing your own Inner Child.

Building Trust

If our Critical or Abandoning Parent has been dominant, our Inner Child may be wary when we begin the re-parenting process. If we have not been in the habit of nurturing our Inner Child, it may take some time to build trust. When addressed by an adult "voice" who says it wants to be "friends," the Child may be skeptical, frightened, angry, or refuse to talk at all.

A wonderful way to build trust with our Inner Child is to write a letter of apology. We admit that we have not taken care of the Child as well as it would have liked. In the examples in previous chapters you saw how the Inner Child, especially the Vulnerable or Angry Child, readily tells us how it has been abused or abandoned by us.

The next exercise is a letter of apology admitting your negligence, manipulation, or abuse of the Inner Child. Most important, it is an opportunity to declare your intention to change your ways by listening to and caring for your Inner Child in all of its aspects. The goal is to build trust and open up loving communication between your Inner Parent and your Inner Child.

MY APOLOGIES

MATERIALS: Paper and pen.

With your dominant hand write a letter of apology to your Inner Child. Ask for the Child's forgiveness for the times when you were overly critical, bossy, impatient, or when you ignored and neglected the Child's needs altogether. Tell your Inner Child that you are learning how to take better care of it, and thank it for sharing feelings and needs with you.

To My Child Within—

Dear Child,

I need to let you know, finally, that I do *love you!* You haven't received what you need from me and I aploogize for that. I *now* know how much this has hurt you and I'm sorry. Maybe it will help if I can explain why things have been this way up till now.

It's simple—I just didn't know that I was neglecting you! Recently, God has blessed me by showing that the way I grew up wasn't healthy. My unhealthy nurturing skills were taught to me by *my* parents. I thougt my skills were O.K. & *normal*! So I treated you just the way my parents raised me. This chain was sick and, from today on, I will do my part to break this cycle. I will take discernable, positive actions to grow in my ability to love & nurture you, as well as others. I pray that you will forgive my past ignorance and now allow me in to your innermost self—where we can play, grow, share, & learn to show our love for each other.

Your loving parent

Dear Inner Child—

I'm not real sure if I am getting in touch with you, but I will try. I felt something last night. I will try harder to get in touch with you, because you are so very important in my life. Taking care of you is the most important thing to do in my life. You are a gift to this planet and I will love you by protecting you and helping share your love with the world. I am so very sorry that you were very abused by mean people. That was so terrible. And, I am sorry that I have pretty much ignored you these past years. I love you and will work hard to take care of you. It will take time and money to work on this. Words can hardly say how much you mean to me. You are the wind in my sails, the sweetness in my day. Without you, I cannot imagine how to live—or why. I feel love for you and from you. I am happy about that. Thank you honey for saying I look pretty today. What a nice thing that was for me to hear today! Because I respect you a lot and know that you are very wise and you know a lot about beauty. I will learn more about how to protect you, for that is my job today. No one else can do it and that is why I have given up trying to get a man to love me. They can't do for me what only I can do for you. I want to know more about what you want and need to feel safe and loved. I won't let people come in the trailer and I will get us away from bad people no matter what. I love you and cherish you and respect you. I hope you feel safe with me. I love you.

Another way to build trust with your Inner Child is to write it a love letter. In workshops I have seen miraculous results with this exercise, especially with people who were severely abused or badly neglected in childhood. Individuals who do not receive nurturing in childhood often find that the prospect of re-parenting themselves looms before them as an overwhelming task. They say things such as: "I don't know what good parenting looks like. How can I re-parent myself if I never learned how by example?"

Their point is well taken. But there is a light in the darkness. It is called love. For no matter how badly we were treated as children, the spirit of love still lives within us and it can be tapped. Even a child like Anne Frank, who was eventually killed by the Nazis in World War II, could write of this love in her own heart. In her diary, written while she and her family were in hiding from the Gestapo, Anne remarked: "In spite of everything, I still believe that people are really good at heart."

As you saw in earlier dialogues, a real opening of the heart occurs when the Inner Child is allowed to speak. That natural, feeling, spontaneous Child is lovable and to know it—truly know it—is to love it. So here's your chance to express love to the Child you discovered in your earlier dialogues. This love letter can heal your Inner Child and it can heal you.

LOVE LETTER TO YOUR INNER CHILD

MATERIALS: Paper, felt pens, and crayons.

1. With your dominant hand, let your Nurturing Parent write a love letter to your very own Inner Child. Tell the Child about all its special and unique qualities, and how much you love it. Tell the Child what you are doing to take good care of it and what you want to do for it in the future.

2. If you have someone in your life with whom you feel safe, ask him or her to read this love letter to your Inner Child aloud to you. Afterward, you may want to share how it felt to receive this message of love.

3. Do a drawing of your Nurturing Parent caring for your Inner Child. Put the picture where you can look at it frequently.

The following letters were written by participants in a weekend retreat for healing the Inner Child:

Dear Inner Child,

I love you. I feel that if you had not been here with me, I could not have been a teacher, especially I could not have done the things I did. The kids would not have responded to me. I am glad for your playfulness but also for your vulnerability. Because of you I responded to that in my students. Of course, I had not recognized you at that time. I had not nurtured that in myself but when I danced in the women's group, you were the one who did the dancing. When I went to the acting class, you were the one who acted. When I was free with the children you were there being me. I love my free child.

I also love my hurt, lonely child. Oh how you wanted to be seen and heard. How you wanted to trust your environment, your parents. You were good but you were pushed and shoved. You were whipped and yelled at. You were told you were no good, that you would never amount to anything but you didn't give up.

I love my rebellious child. Because of you I didn't give up on myself. You were angry because of the tight control. Because of that anger I have—you have—we have power. Still I need to set limits as an adult and as a nourishing parent so that I can do what I need to do. I love you.

Dearest Little One, My Sweetie,

You are a very special little girl. Bright, eager, enthusiastic, full of energy, and laughter. I am so sorry that you are not allowed to express your feelings when you were little & were not allowed to say what you wanted & what you didn't want & have those feelings & want to be respected. As you know, I've been working on setting you free for a long time. I've been working on how to listen to you. What I want you to know is that I intend to pay attention to you. I want you to help me know what I want & what I don't want. I want to integrate you into my life. I want a balanced life. I want to let go of all the anger I've been carrying around with me all my life & learn to express my feelings & wants appropriately, as they arise from now on.

You really did a splendid job in coping with your life as you found it. Thank you for hanging in there & sticking in there & showing me ways to enjoy life all along.

I will listen to you & value your input.
I love you, Little One. Your sense of humor is the best!

The Inner Child does not trust words. It believes in actions. It gets deeply hurt and disappointed when we make promises and then break them. If that happens a lot, the Child hides and carries anger and resentment. Who wouldn't? In the outer world, we build respect and credibility when we keep agreements. The same is true in the world of Inner Parenting. In order to build a trusting relationship, it is essential that we ask the Inner Child what it needs. By listening and then responding appropriately, we show the Child that we mean what we say. We demonstrate that we truly want to take better care of it.

If you find that you have difficulty following through on your promises to the Inner Child, find a support group of some kind. State your goal of re-parenting your Inner Child and get help. You don't have to do this all alone, but you do have to do it for yourself. I have seen miracles in support groups. A weekly group devoted to re-parenting the Inner Child can be of tremendous value in applying the principles presented here. This book can serve as a guide. Also, in my book *The Picture of Health* there is a chapter on how to start a support group. I recommend it as a framework.

As we develop a loving relationship with our own Inner Child, the need to find substitute Nurturing Parents in the outer world diminishes. We no longer put demands on our family or friends to do our Inner Parenting for us. We do it for ourselves. As this happens, relationships begin to transform. In their second book, *Embracing Each Other,* Hal Stone and Sidra Winkel-man describe what happens when we get stuck in negative bonding patterns. According to their Voice Dialogue model, the term *bonding patterns* refers to the ". . . activation of parent/child patterns of interaction between two people. These are normal and natural configurations that exist in all relationships." They go on to say that the "catalyst for all negative bonding patterns is the activation of the disowned vulnerability." In other words, the Vulnerable Child gets disowned by one of the two people and sets off a chain reaction.

For instance, when Mr. Fisher, a highly successful CEO, feels overwhelmed, he goes into a Critical Parent mode and puts pressure on his secretary, Mrs. Clark. She goes into the Dutiful Daughter and works harder, faster, and longer to please her boss. She soon realizes she needs an assistant to help with the greater work load, but does not discuss it with Mr. Fisher. It seems that he is now suffering from hypertension headaches and gets her sympathy. Coming to his rescue from her Nurturing Mother, she avoids asking for what she really needs with the following excuses: "He has so much on his mind. I don't want to trouble him with one more problem. And he's already upset about the budget." Meanwhile, her Inner Child (who lives in the body) is worn out and gets sick. A temporary assistant is hired, but only because Mrs. Clark is now home with the flu for a few days.

If Mrs. Clark's Nurturing Parent had listened to her own Inner Child sooner and gotten her Protective Parent to ask for help in the first place, she might not have become ill. Before we jump to the conclusion that Mr. Fisher would not have authorized hiring temporary assistance, let me point out that she did not even give him a chance. She never asked because she was too busy reading his mind, predicting his reaction, and preventing it from happening. This kind of controlling behavior completely ignores the needs of her Inner Child. And it prevents Mr. Fisher from taking responsibility for his own Inner Child, his feelings and physical well-being. Mrs. Clark got the help she needed after all, but she paid a high price: sickness.

Understanding the dynamics of our Inner Family has far-reaching implications for all of our relationships. As we become conscious of our Inner Child and learn to nurture and protect it, these negative bonding patterns come to light and we can do something about them. As we become aware, we widen our choices.

The next exercise helps you to discover your Inner Child's needs and to respond with an appropriate plan. We cannot give the Child everything it wants all at once. There are other aspects of our lives and other sub-personalities that must be honored, too. However, as with anything else, if we don't make time on the calendar for our Child's requests, they might get overlooked. Then we are back to lots of talk and no action, broken promises and no trust. Being a Nurturing Parent to your Inner Child means being a trustworthy one. When you say you are going to do something, DO IT. No excuses, no rationalizing. Don't make promises that you are not going to keep.

NURTURING YOUR INNER CHILD

MATERIALS: Paper, felt pens, crayons, and your personal calendar.

1. Ask your Inner Child to tell you what kind of nurturing it needs at this time in your life. Let the Child write with your non-dominant hand. Be specific. For instance, the Child might write, "I want to take a walk by the ocean every morning."

2. Writing with the dominant hand, tell the Child how you will specifically respond to its requests.

3. Write the responses into a calendar so that you will not forget to do them. Put these responses into action by including them in your everyday life. For instance:

Monday evening:	Get a massage.
Wednesday afternoon:	Have lunch in the park.
Thursday morning:	Take a bike ride before work.
Saturday morning:	Sleep in, don't do any "have to's" like housework or laundry. Just "hang out" and do nothing.

4. Use your non-dominant hand. Draw a picture of your Nurturing Parent and Inner Child doing one of the activities on your list.

This drawing, done in a workshop, evokes the warmth and love that characterizes the relationship between the Nurturing Parent and Child Within.

Child: I am Faith Ann and I'm your Inner Child. Like I said yesterday, I want you to be nice to me & stop saying mean things to me. And don't let Paul get away with saying mean things either. Do your plan. For every mean thing you hear say 2 nice things about us back. If you hear "You're a sniveler", say I am in touch with my feelins & I am healthy. I want you to stop worrying. You don't need anymore grey hairs or wrinkles. Have more fun. Laugh, laugh, laugh. Ha Ha Ha. HA HA!!! Play more with Nick. Go for walks on trails w/him. Bring him here. Teach Naomi the beadwork like she's been bugging you. You know it's fun. Also go for walks w/Jyenci at night and early in the morning. Morning is better. Starts the day w/love. She loves & admires you as much as you love & admire her. And leave Paul alone. Let me write instead of bugging him to love you. Let me love you. You know. I think you need me to love you just as much as I need you to love me. Let's make a deal & be nice to each other then we don't have to be so sad & serious. HA HA.

This woman pictured her Nurturing Parent dancing with an older Child Within. These drawings were a major breakthrough for her artistic, creative child as she thought she could not draw people.

Following an Inner Child weekend workshop, a woman gave me a note describing her process of finding a Nurturing Parent Within through art and writing:

Two or three weeks ago I created a collage. I started out with the idea of the inner child. The child was kneeling with arms raised to a mother who was a flame with a woman's shape. She had no arms and I was the one who had cut them off. The child was black and charred. They both were rising from an urn. This was only part of the collage.

Feb. 24th in your workshop I drew a picture of the Vulnerable Child and Nurturing Parent. The mother sits (very grounded) with her arms around the child. I kept drawing the arms stronger and stronger. The mother had a rounded shape. The child felt safe and the mother said, "You are my beloved child."

Before doing the new mother/child drawing, this woman had done the following dialogue with her Vulnerable Child. I believe this dialogue, in which she accessed her Nurturing Parent, enabled her to re-picture the parent/child relationship within and to truly embrace her Vulnerable Child.

Adult: You look so sad, I see your tears.

Child: I am sad. I hurt

Adult: Do you want me to hold you?

Child: Yea I need you to take care of me

Adult: I will hold you and take care of you.

Child: I am afraid that you will go away

Adult: I will not go away. I will be more loving to you.

Parent: What do you need from me?

Child: Hold me. I feel safe now. Love me, keep a safe place for me.

Parent: I will do all of these things for you. You are my beloved child.

N.P. — What do you need from me?
V.C. — Hold me.   I feel safe now
         Love me.   keep a safe place for me
N.P. — I will do all
of these things
for you.
you are my
beloved child.

A NURTURING PERSON

MATERIALS: Paper, crayons, and felt pens.

1. Think about someone whom you felt loved and nurtured by at some time in your life. It may have been a spouse, relative, a neighbor, or a friend. It may also be someone like a teacher or a therapist.

2. Ask your Inner Child to draw a picture of you and this person. Show a time when you felt nurtured by this person. Do the drawing with your non-dominant hand.

3. Write a dialogue. Let your Inner Child (with your non-dominant hand) tell how it felt RECEIVING love and nurturance. Let the nurturing person tell how it felt to GIVE love to you.

4. If there is something troubling you at this time, let your Inner Child tell what it is with the non-dominant hand. Then let the nurturing person from the past respond with your non-dominant hand.

Allan Nicholson's Story

To illustrate the Inner Parent in action, I would like to share Allan's story. Allan and I met at the LA Center for Living, where I was leading workshops. The LA Center was a lovely home where support services were offered for persons with AIDS and other life-threatening or chronic illnesses. Allan, who was volunteering his time and making a video documentary on the center's services, attended my Inner Child workshop. We did not meet again until a month later. This time Allan was with his mother, who had flown to California from Boston. They told me an incredible story.

Since attending his first Inner Child workshop, Allan had become ill with pneumocystis and was taken to Los Angeles County General Hospital. He was diagnosed with AIDS. County General Hospital is a gigantic prison-like building. As a publicly-funded hospital, it has a reputation for being over-crowded, understaffed, a frightening place to visit even when one is well.

You certainly would not want to take your Vulnerable Inner Child there. But Allan was taken there when he became ill. And the amazing thing is that, in spite of the grim environment, his stay there became a blissful experience.

When he told me this, I was incredulous. How could this be? Allan went on to explain that he entered into dialogue with his Inner Child while in the hospital. At first he was too ill to write the conversations, but he had learned how to access his Inner Child. So he kept having mental dialogues and asking his Inner Child what he needed. Actually, it was Allan's Inner Nurturing Parent who was asking the Child what he needed. More important, Allan's Protective Parent made sure that he communicated to the nurses and doctors what he needed.

The love that poured out of his Inner Child when it was allowed to show itself drew so much caring back from others that Allan could speak about his hospitalization as "bliss." He recovered from the pneumocystis and was enthusiastic about sharing his experience with others. After he told his story, I understood, for I have seen how the Vulnerable Child softens the hearts of others and draws to it a showering of love. Allan told about receiving a stuffed animal (for his Inner Child) and tender, loving care from family, friends, hospital staff, and even other patients.

Allan, an entertainer, went on to do several one-man shows in Los Angeles in which his Inner Child did some songs. One of these numbers was "Slippy, Sloppy, Flippy, Floppy Shoes," in which Allan wore swim fins (simulating a child wearing adult's shoes). He received a standing ovation at the performance I attended. The audience was visibly moved by Allan's adorable little Inner Child, who turned out to be a genuine show-stopper.

Nearly two years after his original diagnosis, Allan died of AIDS. My close friend Cassandra Christenson, called me with the news. Former education director of the L.A. Center for Living, Cassandra is a nurse who helps midwife the dying. She does this by actually coaching them through the moment of death. She was present when Allan passed away, and said the scene was identical to one Allan had pictured in his mind during his first hospitalization. He was surrounded by people he loved and who loved him: his mother, sister, and friends. I was deeply touched when she said: "Lucia,

Allan looked like a small child at the moment of his death. His mother and sister were holding him and he went in total peace. It was beautiful for all of us." I later spoke with Allan's mother. She said the same thing. Her experience of her son's death was one of peace and love.

Loving Your Angry Child

As I mentioned in Chapter 4, the Angry Child Within is one of the most difficult for us to accept. But a Nurturing Parent can do this. After accessing the Nurturing Parent Within it becomes easier to express love to our Inner Child in *all* its moods: when it is sad, hurt, happy, or mad. It is common to see several different emotions expressed by the Child in the course of a written dialogue. The calm and stabilizing quality of the Nurturing Parent voice allows the Inner Child to be itself, especially when it is angry. Safely venting anger helps the Child move on to other feelings. In the following dialogue you will see a rapport developing between a woman's Nurturing Parent and her Angry Child. The Child's feelings change often during the dialogue, from angry, to happy, to sad, to angry, to happy and loved.

Adult: Hello little girl. What's your name.

Child: My name is Alice. No! My name is anger. And I'm mad because they gave that name to my sister.

Adult: How stupid of them.

Child: Yes.

Adult: Well, I can call you Amy. Would you like that?

Child: Yes.

Adult: Amy dear, how old are you?

Child: I am 8 years old—maybe 5.

Adult: What do you like to do?

Child: I like to ride my bike draw pictures & look out of windows.

Adult: Amy dear, what do you like to do in your house?

Child: I have to be quiet because mommy & daddy fight about me.

Adult: How do you feel when they fight?

Child: I feel bad. That I'm a bad girl—and I am all alone & that Mommy and daddy are pulling me apart.

Adult: I'm sorry you feel bad. You're not a bad girl at all. You're a darling little girl.

Child: Am I?

Adult: Yes, you're a darling darling little girl & I love you very very much. Amy, what don't you like to do?

Child: I don't like to go to Grandmas house because it smells bad, I'm ignored, & I feel sad around grandma & mommy.

Adult: Can you tell mommy that?

Child: No!

Adult: What do you feel now?

Child: I feel happy & sad.

Adult: Why do you feel happy?

Child: I just do.

Adult: Can you tell me why you feel sad?

Child: She dressed me up as an ugly witch & at camp she dressed me like a maid & sent me to a goyim school. why didn't she dress me up as a princess. She's stupid & ugly & I hate her.

Adult: Amy, Amy what would you like now?

Child: I would like to kill her.

Adult: Amy, It's okay to be angry & I'm going to be with you no matter how you feel.

Child: Thank you.

Adult: My pleasure. I'm happy to be with you. What would you like now?

Child: I want a pretty dress and pretty clothes & an eclair & a Charlotte russe and I want a mommy & daddy to love me.

Adult: Amy, Amy honey child how can I help you? What can I do for you?

Child: be with me. don't leave me alone - massage me

Adult: Amy what would you like for lunch?

Child: A warm soup & sweet dessert.

Adult: Amy darling, I will give you what you want within my power & I will be with you and never leave you & I'll massage you tonite.

Child: I'm happy I have someone who loves me and will take care of me.

Adult: Amy, I need to go now but I'll come back soon and spiritually I'll always be with you.

Child: I wish I could believe you.

Adult: You can darling. You're me. Amy dear, I know you don't want to risk hurting this time and darling that's *okay.* You can stay where you are for as long as you like.

Child: I'm glad to hear that.

Pre-Birth Bonding

Behold, children are a gift of the Lord.
PSALM 127:3

A topic that has been receiving some attention in recent years is pre-birth bonding: connecting emotionally with the being who is in the process of entering life on the planet. My first experience with this happened when I discovered I was pregnant with my first child. Upon returning home from the doctor's office, I wrote a poem. Later I made a large collage mural on which I printed the poem:

> *Who are you*
> *who shall call me mother*
> *placing on my head*
> *that glorious crown*
> *tied with the love knot?*

I remember the feeling of connecting deeply with a being who had chosen me for its mother in this human life. It was a new idea: that my child had chosen me to be its mother. I had always heard people complain about their parents, saying, "Look, I didn't ask to be born." But in writing that poem, somehow I knew I had been chosen. And I felt honored and bonded to this new life.

Twenty-seven years later my youngest daughter became pregnant with her first child. In thinking about being a grandparent, I wanted to know why my grandchild was coming into the world. So with my dominant hand I posed the question, and with my non-dominant hand the child responded: "I'm coming in to bring love." He certainly has done that.

Several years ago, one of my readers wrote that she was adapting some of my journal techniques in her work as a childbirth educator. Sandra Bardsley has been teaching birth-preparation classes in which the parents keep journals. In these journals they express their feelings about having a child, they write about their own births (based on what they have been told), and they visualize the kind of birth experience they want. Sandra feels that this journaling process has helped many women deal with the birth pain and maximize their natural childbirth experience.

In working with a group that included several young mothers, I described the technique of dialoguing with the unborn child. One of the mothers, Carol, was pregnant with her second child. She decided to do a right/left-hand dialogue with the child. Her fascinating dialogue appears here. Her son was born several weeks later.

Adult: Hello little child inside of me. I hope you know that I love you, I want to see you, hold you, nurse you, know you more then I do but I also want you to wait until we are settled back in Martha's Vineyard before you are born. Do you feel my love? Will you wait?

Child: Is there room for me in your life? I am another teacher for you. You know me already - that is one reason you are not in a hurry for me to be born. You need to let go of your attachment for me to be a boy. I embrace the female and male sides. You can enjoy both qualities if you are open to seeing both in one sex. You do not want a girl because you associate that with you. Your deep rooted disapproval of yourself and your conditioned bias towards boys creates a prejudice against girls. I know you will do love me but, the judging is damaging your own self image.

Adult: Thank you for telling me all of that. I embrace your qualities already. There is room for you in my life. I will make room, more room for you, and for me. Why did you choose Paul and me as your parents? How will it help you and me in our life paths?

Child: Amara (older sibling in the family) said it. She has a wisdom but she needs help to know her own power. She needs someone to boost her up, and give her purpose. It is my time for a place of security. There is very little of that around. You can give a safe place, love, family, no financial insecurities. Yet it is also an unsure place. How both of your lives will evolve. It talks of change and new awareness. Keep the process alive with Paul or else it will all die.

Healing the Pain of Childlessness

For many years, Sue had harbored a deep sadness about not being able to be a mother. A happily married artist living in Japan, Sue found my book *The Power of Your Other Hand* and began doing Inner Child dialogues. Sue came to the realization that she was very hurt about never having had children. She had always loved kids and wanted several of her own, but had married at thirty-seven and had a history of female problems. Sue was never able to get pregnant, and by the time she and her husband thought of adoption it felt too late because of his age.

Rather than feel sorry for herself, Sue decided to become involved with children on her own. At that point she was presented with several opportunities. She began working with Japanese kids, who she found to be very special and loving. In a letter to me, she wrote:

> Several weeks ago at our Christmas party, I cried as I was asked to express my thoughts about working with these kids. They had given more to me than I had given to them.

Around this time, Sue's husband bought her a video camera. She had fallen in love with the Japanese children and wanted to sketch them. So out she went into the streets of Kamakura, where she found great crowds of school-children and pre-schoolers with their mothers. She began making videos of these kids wherever she saw them playing games, dancing, singing, and reading their books. She would then watch the videos over and over again to study the children's movements. By freeze-framing she could capture their motions and sketch them. Sue included the following drawing of Japanese children in her letter.

In reflecting upon her experiences, Sue continued to write:

> While I would still love to have children of my own, I have found the best substitute—enjoying other people's. I enjoy the spontaneity, joy and exuberance, the endless surprises, and the endless action of children in their everyday lives—responding to their friends, their environment, and their own inner energy. I actually see the parts of the children that the parents never see—while they are away from the confines and conflicts of family life and school, and just free to be themselves. What fun I have had and how lucky I am!

Without having her own children, Sue has developed the kind of healthy, nurturing attitude I have been discussing in this chapter. In this way she has been healing herself. After many months of healing work she wrote this poem and drew a picture of her Inner Child.

POEM FROM MY PARENT SELF TO MY INNER CHILD
(I have to be a mother-father to my inner child)

You are beautiful and good my child—
Walk tall and straight and proud—
Proud to be yourself.
For there is only one You.
You are like a bright shining diamond
Shining like the moon
Gleaming bright like stars at night
Sending radiance to all around.
Walk straight my child and feel
Feel the song of our love in
Your ears and heart and in your (belly) womb.
Let it mend and heal and touch all parts
And give you a warm and loving heart.''

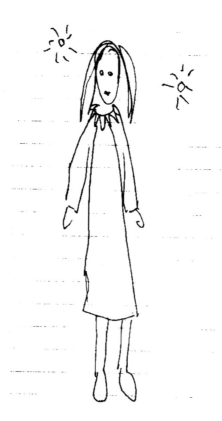

Sue's last comments, about being able to see what parents do not see, brings up the dilemma of being a parent. Having raised two children myself, I certainly know that it is often difficult to keep one's own Inner Child alive while being a "responsible" parent to children in the outer world. But it is our Inner Child that enables us as parents to truly understand and resonate with our children. So if you are a parent—or a grandparent—you can use the techniques in this book to keep nurturing your own Inner Child.

I can say from personal experience that as I re-parented myself, my relationship with my daughters improved dramatically. I was able to relax and really enjoy them, while still being a responsible adult. I am especially pleased to see my daughters interact with my grandchildren. They have a deep respect for these little beings, because they are aware of their own Inner Child.

AWARENESS

With your dominant hand write down your reactions to this chapter on the Nurturing Parent. Without criticizing or analyzing, review any work that you did. Briefly summarize what happened in your art and writing. What did you discover? Have you noticed your Nurturing Parent being active in your everyday life? In what situations? In what areas does your Inner Child most need your Nurturing Parent Within?

PROTECTIVE PARENT
PROTECT VULNERABLE
CHILD

SIX

Invoking the Protective Parent

Unlike reptiles (who are born fully developed and capable of fending for themselves), we humans cannot survive infancy and childhood on our own. We need to be fed, clothed, and sheltered. We need to be nurtured and protected, both physically and emotionally. This is true for the Inner Child as well. In Chapter 5, we explored a caring relationship between the Nurturing Parent and the Child Within. But parenting is incomplete without protection.

The image of a protector archetype is as old as human culture. We see it in the tribesman who marks out his territory and protects it from invasion by outsiders. The protective instinct is illustrated in the earliest cave paintings portraying human beings facing the awesome power of animals. Folklore and religious literature are peopled with heroes whose victories depend on activating protective forces, without as well as within. By invoking the protection of the gods, as well as developing their own inner courage, these humans became heroes. They rose above the vulnerability of the human condition.

In the Judeo-Christian tradition we have the stories of Noah and the flood, David and Goliath, and Jonah and the Whale as examples of mere humans dealing with giants and the overwhelming power of nature. Like the child heroes of fairy tales, these biblical figures triumphed over seemingly impossible challenges. And later the theme of Christ's life shows us victory over death and the promise of eternal life. In European literature, the archetype of the protector appears in the legend of Arthur. The symbols of the knight—sword, shield, armor, and horse—epitomize protective power. In modern times, we have Luke Skywalker (the young hero of *Star Wars*), battling the evil and heavily armored Darth Vader.

These tales continue to fascinate us because they speak of universal truths. They dramatize the dynamics of the individual psyche. For we each have an inner protector at work who ensures our survival. In modern psychology the protector of the psyche has been given many names. Freud labeled it the Superego. Jung spoke of it as the Persona. More recently, in Transactional Analysis, it has been called the Parent. In Voice Dialogue this sub-personality is known as the Protector-Controller.

We all have a Protector. Without one we would not survive beyond childhood. However, the Protector may eventually operate self-destructively in adult life. What might have worked in childhood as a survival strategy may damage or even endanger the quality of one's life in adulthood. For instance, when a child has to deal with abusive and violent parents, a protective self may have to hide the Inner Child. It may have to erect a wall of defenses, or numb the Inner Child's feelings with addictive substances, compulsive behavior, or illness. All of these mood-altering states help to keep the Inner Child's feelings hidden, from the self and others.

The Protector in us is a security guard whose job is survival. It protects us by scoping out the rules and regulations of the environment and allowing safe and appropriate behavior. The Protector operates within the context of family and culture. Early on it learns what is acceptable in the eyes of others who matter. It also learns what is unacceptable and what will lead to trouble (punishment, disapproval, abandonment, etc). The Protector attempts to control the environment in order to eliminate the feeling or appearance of helplessness.

In a dysfunctional family where it was dangerous for the Inner Child to express feelings, heavy protection may have been necessary. For instance, it may not have been safe to let vulnerability or anger show. Many adult survivors of child abuse tell about how they were threatened or punished severely if they cried after being abused. Parents commanded them to "stop crying or I will *really* give you something to cry about!" The tragedy is that self-protection through numbness, emotional armoring, escape, or withdrawal actually damages the Inner Child, especially its vulnerable aspect.

If we did not grow up with examples of *healthy* protective parenting in our environment, then we need to cultivate that ability in ourselves. This may appear difficult (or even impossible), but it can be done. It is an essential aspect of re-parenting. This chapter offers tools for contacting and developing a healthy Protective Parent Within.

The Protective Parent

I have discovered an aspect of the psyche whose job it is to look out for our Inner Child's welfare. I call this the Protective Parent. This sub-personality is not to be confused with the Protector-Controller of Voice Dialogue, Freud's Superego, or any other equivalent. *The Protective Parent is a child's rights advocate.* It tunes in to the Child's level of safety or threat and senses its need for protection. The Protective Parent sets boundaries and limits. It deals with others who would cross those boundaries, either intentionally or through ignorance. It handles the outer world when the Inner Child is at risk of being hurt or abandoned.

In order to guard the safety of the Inner Child, the Protective Parent must be in touch with the Child's true needs. That is why developing a Nurturing Parent/Child relationship (as we did in the last chapter) is so important. The Nurturing Parent—with gentleness, understanding, and compassion—makes it safe for the Child to tell honestly how it feels and what it needs. But it is the Protective Parent who takes a stand in the world, who acts in the Child's behalf.

In written dialogues, people's Vulnerable Child often says it feels abandoned, exposed, and unsafe. It talks about wanting protection from the outer world. There may be intimidating authority figures out there and the Inner Child needs to know that there is a Parent Within who can deal effectively with them. It needs an adult who can speak up and communicate, one who can get the Child out of a destructive relationship if need be. But if the Protective Parent does not know what the Child needs, then it cannot do its job.

Ted's boss, Mr. Clayton, was a highly critical, driven individual. He blamed Ted for anything and everything that went wrong in the office, calling him names and putting him down in front of the rest of the staff. Although Ted was a very conscientious worker, he put up with Clayton's scapegoating. Ted had been raised by an extremely impatient, perfectionist stepfather. Ted was used to being judged harshly and blaming himself. In this work situation he reproduced his early family experience and fell into a negative bonding pattern. Clayton played the critical father to his dutiful son. This was an outer reflection of Ted's Inner Family in which his own Inner Critical Parent kept him feeling shamed and "bad."

Ted's Inner Child felt utterly abandoned, however, and the only way it could express itself was through back problems. He was in physical pain much of the time. In a weekly therapy group, Ted's Vulnerable Child was able to draw a picture of itself as an infant/prisoner in chains, waiting to be liberated. In written dialogues, the Inner Child said the back pain would leave when Ted had spine enough to stand up for himself and refuse to bow down under the boss's treatment. After a good deal of re-parenting, Ted was able to confront Clayton and eventually get what his Inner Child wanted all along: a new position working with an employer who appreciated his abilities. Prior to this Ted had not felt worthy of having a satisfying job. As he learned to protect and care for his Inner Child, he was able to shield him from further mistreatment.

A similar process of developing the Protective Inner Parent is necessary for individuals in abusive marriages or intimate relationships. In the case of Phil, whose wife insulted and berated him in public on a regular basis, a strong negative bonding pattern had become habitual. Phil's mother had been an extremely abusive woman, both verbally and physically. It was as if Phil did not know how to relate to any other type of woman. His survival strategy included addiction to pharmaceutical drugs, workaholism, and other obsessive-compulsive behavior. It took a great deal of re-parenting and several 12-step recovery programs for Phil to realize that he did not have to subject himself to such mistreatment. By developing a strong Protective Parent, he was able to set limits on his own compulsive behavior and on his wife's abuse. He left the relationship and eventually created a new healthy one based on a mutual respect for his Inner Child, as well as his partner's.

Much of the work that goes on in shelters for abused women and children involves education in self-protection. The first step is to get the woman out of the household where the abuse is occurring. By providing a safe place, the staff helps the woman experience protection first, so that some nurturing can occur. Abused women need someone to set an example for both nurturance and protection. However, it is absolutely essential that an abused woman learn to contact her own Protective Parent Within. If not, she will return to the destructive situation and once again subject her Inner Child (as well as her actual children) to more violence and abuse. Re-parenting has been an extremely valuable tool for freeing both men and women caught in the clutches of a destructive relationship.

The Protective Parent is a warrior in us. It is directed and focused. It has a purpose. Active and impersonal, the Protective Parent "takes care of business." It does what it has to do in order to safeguard the Inner Child. Unlike the Protector-Controller, who may engage in old survival behavior that ignores the Inner Child's needs, the Protective Parent is always asking, "Is this situation (or relationship) in the best interest of my Inner Child?"

The Protective Parent is unwilling to believe in a False Self who ignores the Inner Child's real needs. Since the Protective Parent voice is impersonal and unsentimental, it is often interpreted as being "selfish." Actually, it is self-interested. It has to be. Its job is to ensure the safety and integrity of the Inner Child. It wants the Child to be itself and to have a home within the Inner Family. The Protective Parent makes it safe for our Inner Child to be seen and heard, first by us and then by others. It protects us appropriately.

The Protective Parent within us is a strong force in breaking the chains of co-dependence. The unemotional nature of this voice allows us to say "no" firmly to people who try to control and manipulate us. It does not get emotionally pulled into other people's problems that they need to resolve for themselves. It does not go running compulsively to the rescue. Rather, it serves the Inner Child and protects it from harm.

Knowing our boundaries and limits is a function of a healthy Protective Parent. For those who were raised in dysfunctional families, boundaries and limit-setting are important issues. This is true for those who had overprotective or controlling caregivers as well as for those who suffered abuse or were abandoned. Under the guise of having the child's best interest at heart, overprotective parents hover like surveillance helicopters or smother the child with demands and pressures. As one man put it, "My mother was all over me like a blanket, always prying and meddling in my life."

Overprotective parents themselves have an abandoned and terrified Inner Child. They see the world through fear-colored glasses, obsess about all manner of real or imagined dangers. What results is an atmosphere of anxiety and vigilance in the home. Such parents never cease to remind their children about the menaces lurking around every corner. They make mountains out of molehills and create chronic tension in the child. This is not healthy protectiveness. It is CONTROL. It usually creates submissiveness and depression in the child, active rebellion, or a pattern of over-responsibility in which the child takes care of the parent.

This kind of controlling behavior can literally drive others to drink, drugs, etc. After all, it is like living with the CIA, the FBI, and the local police all wrapped up in one. Instead of being there to "protect and serve," the overprotective parent disempowers others, making them feel incapable of managing their own lives or taking care of themselves.

Children of overprotective parents may suffer as much as children who were neglected or physically violated. They grow up without developing healthy boundaries, so their boundaries become very fuzzy. They are used to being swallowed up and given no privacy or separateness. They may wear a suit of armor to defend against invasion of their personal space. In close relationships many of these individuals flip back and forth between two extremes: fusing with others prematurely and then pushing them away abruptly. Either way there is rigidity, reactiveness, and a sense of not having a choice in the matter. This relationship pattern becomes a habit that is repeated compulsively over and over again. The development of both a Nurturing Parent and Protective Parent Within can help to change this compulsive pattern.

Needless to say, survivors of child abuse and neglect are sorely in need of protection. Again, they will need to look for and find it inside. Otherwise they can spend a lifetime looking for someone else to be their Protective Parent. This freezes them in the role of helpless victim and never gets to the roots of their feelings of abandonment and emptiness.

Protecting Your Inner Child in Therapy

As you re-parent yourself you may decide to expand your support system. You may consider individual therapy or a group. There are thousands of support groups of all kinds throughout the U.S. and other countries. Some of them, like Adult Children of Alcoholics, are based on the 12-step principles of Alcoholics Anonymous. There are other groups sponsored by therapists and treatment centers. I recommend that you explore such support systems for your healing.

If you discover the need for professional help or a support group, *be sure your Vulnerable Child feels safe with your choice of therapist or group.* How do you know if your Vulnerable Child feels safe? It is simple. *Ask it.* Do a right/left-hand dialogue. Consult with your Inner Child. Ask how it feels about any particular therapist, counseling method, or self-help group you are considering.

Regarding therapy, I caution you to examine the credentials, experience, and integrity of any professional from whom you seek help. Unethical behavior on the part of therapists and doctors is not uncommon. I say this not to discredit the psychological and medical professions or to scare you, but because I have done counseling with both men and women who were abused by therapists, either sexually or emotionally. If your Vulnerable Child is especially fragile, you may be open to being taken advantage of by unscrupulous and unconscious "helpers." Health care professionals are human beings, and unfortunately some of them are in desperate need of healing themselves. Having a lot of initials after their names is no guarantee that professionals are healed themselves. Get referrals from other professionals you trust. Talk to individuals you know who have had therapy and can recommend their therapist.

In seeking out Inner Child seminars, be selective. I have received reports about individuals with insufficient psychological training and little or no clinical experience who purport to lead "Inner Child work." Unfortunately, as Inner Child healing gains in popularity, we will probably see more of these quasi-professionals getting involved. It will be important for those in need of healing to exercise caution and discrimination in their choice of health care practitioners.

Sometimes abuse happens under the guise of "therapeutic techniques." It often appears as intimidation. It may be in the form of emotional or physical seduction that meets the therapist's own distorted needs. Any client who already has problems setting boundaries and protecting him or herself from invasion can easily be manipulated with intellectual "fast talk." Survivors of child abuse are especially vulnerable when it comes to personal boundary issues. In the case of sex between a health care professional and client, it is NEVER justifiable, just as family incest never is. In fact, the two situations are parallel. Both involve victimization of a "child" who has been entrusted to the care of another whose role is to guide, nurture, and protect. In the case of professional incest (sex between a health care professional and client), the child is the client's Vulnerable Child Within.

It is the responsibility of health care professionals to safeguard ethical boundaries between themselves and their clients. However, clients also need to become informed and be discriminating in their choice of a therapist. Developing a strong Protective Parent is especially important in this regard. A Protective Parent is also valuable once an individual is in therapy or in a support group of any kind. In some situations a client may feel that the therapist is trying to push beyond the Inner Child's limits. There is a big difference between encouragement and pressure to perform for the thera-pist's gratification.

After reading some books and talking to others with similar experiences, Sheryl realized that she needed to reclaim her lost childhood. She attended an Inner Child workshop. During a sharing session she told about a therapy group she had recently joined. Before getting into the group, Sheryl told the therapist that she had been raised by high-achieving and extremely de-manding parents who never let her be a child. The therapist assured her that he was experienced in Inner Child work. However, after the third group session, Sheryl began feeling very uncomfortable. It seemed that the ther-apist almost demanded that the group members let all their feelings out and hold nothing back. He did not seem satisfied unless a group member was crying, screaming, stomping, or beating up pillows. If an individual did not express him or herself in this manner, the therapist became critical and allowed other group members to be very judgmental.

In my workshop, Sheryl dialogued with her Vulnerable Child, who wanted a safe place to do her healing work. She did not feel safe when she believed demands were being placed on her to perform for the therapist and group. In the workshop, Sheryl role-played the situation. She was able to let a Protective Parent voice speak out about the lack of safety. Some weeks later, Sheryl wrote me a note of thanks. She had expressed her true feelings in the group. A few others were harboring similar feelings but had gone along with the group because they thought "that was the way therapy was sup-posed to be." Sheryl left the group. She found another group where she continued to do Inner Child dialogues on her own, and began making much healthier choices in her life.

Sheryl's experience reminded me of one I had many years ago. While attending a lecture on the Inner Child, I had to decide whether to take the weekend workshop that followed. Everyone seated around me was caught up in the enthusiasm of the moment. They were all registering for the weekend and expected me to do the same. My "Studious Professional" sub-personality would certainly have signed up. However, I told my friends that I needed to be alone with my Inner Child and find out what she wanted.

Upon returning home, I wrote a dialogue. My Inner Child told me in no uncertain terms that she did not want to go to the workshop. She hated the windowless, fluorescently lit room where the workshop was being held. She did not feel safe with large crowds of people and did not trust the sponsoring group, who she said were "all grown-up and didn't have any Child showing."

Needless to say, I did not take the workshop. However, a close friend and colleague of mine did. Her experience confirmed my Inner Child's gut instinct. Apparently, there were too many participants for the amount of supervision available. People opened up a lot of emotional pain, but there was inadequate guidance from professionals. Many participants were left feeling very vulnerable and raw at the end of the weekend, with no place to process what happened to them.

I cannot place enough emphasis on the importance of the Protective Parent in the re-parenting process. Our Inner Child will simply not feel safe to express all of its feelings and needs unless it knows there is a strong yet caring part of us present. The Child needs to know that we will not sell it down the river and give in to coercion or intimidation from others.

Without a Protective Parent, our Inner Child is truly lost. For a powerful portrait of this lost Inner Child, see the movie *Clean and Sober.* At the end of the film, Michael Keaton (who plays a recovering cocaine addict) tries to convince his woman friend not to return to her abusive mate. In a heart-rending phone conversation with her mate, we watch the woman (Kathy Baker) cave in as she submits to her violator's intimidation. Without a Protective Inner Parent she simply cannot stand up to the bullying of this addictive man. The return to her destructive relationship costs the woman her life in a car accident.

If you have not sensed a Protective Parent within yourself, the task of finding one may seem difficult. For anyone struggling with co-dependence, this sub-personality seems almost alien. However, in order to take responsibility for our own lives and let others do the same, it is essential that we learn to safeguard the Inner Child while at the same time honoring its needs.

DRAWING OUT YOUR PROTECTIVE PARENT

MATERIALS: Paper, felt pens, and crayons.

Draw a picture of your Protective Parent and Inner Child. In your drawing show the Parent protecting the Child from harm or pressure from the outer world. Use your dominant hand.

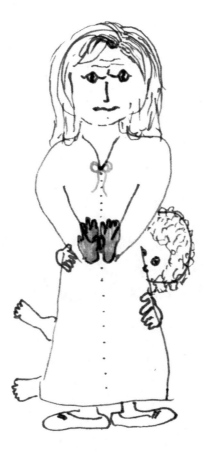

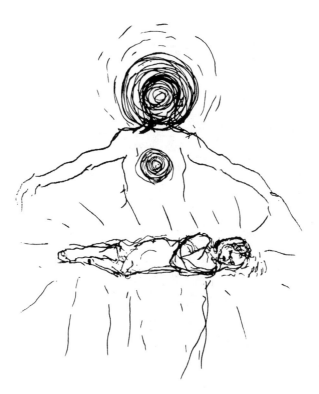

TALKING TO YOUR PROTECTIVE PARENT

1. Write a dialogue in which your Inner Child (non-dominant hand) tells you in which areas of your life it needs protection. Ask the Child to be specific. For instance, Joan's Inner Child wrote:

    I don't like it when the boss calls you names. I feel bad. I don't like being called stupid. It's o.k. to make a mistake & admit it but I don't have to be called names. I want you to tell him that. He had no right to name-call. He can point out a mistake so you can correct it, but don't call me names. If he does, I'll go on strike. I'll get sick or something so I won't have to go to work and listen to him being mean. I mean it!!!

2. After doing the dialogue, with your non-dominant hand draw a picture of your Protective Parent and Inner Child. In the picture show the Parent protecting the Child in one of the situations it

described above. Show how the Parent protects the Child. What does it do or say in order to take care of the Child's needs?

Protective Parent: Role-Playing

Role-playing is a therapeutic technique that has been around for a long time. There are many versions of it and entire methods of therapy that rely on dramatization. Moreno's Psychodrama was one of the first modalities to use dramatic re-creations of real-life relationships and situations. Gestalt Therapy, developed by Fritz Perls, employs spoken dialogues in which the client plays himself, parts of himself, and other people or elements in his life. Virginia Satir developed a variety of role-play techniques in her work with family systems. And, of course, Voice Dialogue calls for an acting out of the individual's sub-personalities.

Role-playing real-life situations with a safe person can be extremely valuable. This is especially true when you are developing a Protective Parent Within who must deal with the outer world. Role-playing can be done in individual therapy, in a group, or in a workshop setting. If you have never done it before, it is best to do it under the guidance of someone who is experienced in role-playing. If you have experience in role-playing, you might want to try it in conjunction with the written dialogue work in this chapter. Be sure you select a role-play partner who is safe and who will not criticize or judge you.

ROLE-PLAY

Think of a situation or a relationship in your life where your Inner Child needs protection. This may be a relationship with an abusive family member, neighbor, coworker, employer, landlord, etc. Describe this situation or relationship to your role-play partner. In the role-play your job is to play yourself in the situation. Ask your role-play partner to play the part of that individual in your life from whom your Inner Child wants to be protected.

The following is a role-play based on the dialogue Joan had with her Inner Child, shown in the last exercise:

Boss: This work is terrible. It's completely unacceptable. I can't believe that you could turn this in to me.

Joan: Uh, uh, um. I'm sorry, but uh,uh, I thought. . . . . .

Boss: I don't see any sign of thinking in this work. I see stupidity. You're just careless, that's all.

Joan: Uh, um, uh, I was just doing what I thought I was supposed to, uh, uh. . . . . . . I don't know. . . . . . .

Boss: Well I don't know either. What I see here is laziness and disorganization.

(Realizing that her supervisor is coming from the Critical Parent and that she has been stuck in her Vulnerable Child feeling threatened, Joan suddenly shifts into an awareness of her Protective Parent, who does not want the Vulnerable Child to be called names.)

Joan: Mrs. Carlson, I've been doing the best I can with the guidelines that I received. I want to do a good job. But it looks like I need more information from you.

Boss: What kind of information?

Joan: I need to know specifically where the mistakes are so that I can correct them.

Boss: Oh, I see. (Flustered, pauses) Well, uh, let's see. (Pause) Come to my office and I'll show you where the errors are.

In the role-play, when Joan shifted into her Protective Parent voice, it took the wind right out of the boss's sails. The person playing the boss really backed down. She had no place to dump her put-downs and name-calling because Joan was not taking it anymore. The shift in energy is very subtle and quite powerful. When we change sub-personalities it has a strong effect on others.

Symbols of Protection

From time immemorial, human beings have crafted artifacts that symbolized power and protection. Whether in the form of talismans that were worn on the body or totems that were carried or erected as large sculptured forms, power symbols appear in the art and architecture of all cultures. This need to acknowledge a higher power that can protect us from harm has also been ritualized in dances and ceremonies. One film of a Native American tribe shows the dance of elder mothers in a ritual of protection. Their sons had been sent away to the armed services and they were invoking the spirits to send them back safely. Each woman carried a large handcrafted, shield-like form. The only boy in the tribe who did not return alive was the one whose family failed to participate in the ceremony.

The creative imagination can be a powerful resource for accessing the inner protection we have and need. We can find a personal symbol like a totem or talisman that can be an effective reminder of protection for our Inner Child. The following exercise shows you how to connect with your own personal power object or image.

A PORTRAIT OF PROTECTION

MATERIALS: Paper, felt pens, and crayons (pastels or colored pencils).

1. With your non-dominant hand, let your Inner Child draw a symbolic portrait of protection. Use any image that feels right to you.

One woman drew a chambered nautilus shell (shown on the following page). Other people have pictured caves, nests, transparent bubbles, animals, rocks, trees, magic shields, etc. It is important that your Child find its own unique symbol of protection.

2. Still using your non-dominant hand, ask your Inner Child to write about what kind of protection it needs from that image or symbol in the drawing. The qualities of the image came out of the Child's creative imagination. Those particular qualities are obviously significant at this particular time. Let the Child tell you what they are.

3. Use this image or symbol as a focus for meditation or at times when you need to invoke your Protective Parent.

The following picture of a nautilus shell and the accompanying Inner Child writing were done by a woman at a workshop. She used her non-dominant hand.

MY PORTRAIT OF PROTECTION

To my protection:

I need you to help me to allow enough water in my life to allow me to grow but I need you to protect me from getting engulfed and/or drowning.

I need the wisdom from you and the awareness to know when I'm in danger.

I need you to help me set boundaries and limits but to be flexible.

I need you to come behind me and prop me up when my roots are weak.

I need you to keep the sand from washing away from under me.

I need you to hide me in your deepest chamber when I'm in danger and not tell anyone where I am.

I need to trust that you will always be there for me.

I need one of your chambers to store my fruit and seeds.

Protection From a Higher Power

The theme of protection can be seen in all religions and spiritual traditions. A classic example is found in the words of the Lord's Prayer: "... And deliver us from evil ..." In prayer an individual often asks for divine protection against danger in the outside world, but he or she might also ask for protection against the tendency to avoid personal responsibility. Although not a religion, 12-Step programs include prayer and meditation as a means for connecting with one's Higher Power.

Many years ago I conducted a weekend retreat for ninety-five women—all recovering alcoholics. The retreat consisted of extended journaling periods interspersed with open sharing. The most moving part of the weekend came at the very end. The group wrote dialogues with their Higher Power and asked for help and protection in their recovery process. When they read their dialogues out loud, these women literally glowed. They told of experiencing—for the first time—that the Higher Power resided inside themselves. Prior to that, many had thought the Higher Power lived in some distant place. These women were raised in dysfunctional families. Many of them were survivors of severe neglect or abuse. As they described the feeling of protection that came with experiencing the Higher Power *inside* them, many of the women wept. They had found a part of themselves that had been lost—a power that would always be there when they needed it. All they had to do was call upon it and trust that it would be there.

In an Inner Child workshop for persons with AIDS and other life-threatening diseases, I wanted to demonstrate our relationship with our Higher Power. I happened to be holding my own teddy bear: a light brown Momma bear holding her baby. We had been discussing the Nurturing Parent and Protective Parent, so I pointed out that the Momma and baby represented the Nurturing Parent embracing the Inner Child. But without protection, that baby was still in danger. So I reached over and picked up a larger brown grizzly bear who was sitting on a nearby sofa. It looked like a Protective Parent who could definitely defend the Momma and baby bear against danger. I placed the Momma and baby in the grizzly bear's lap. The group was very pleased. However, I pointed out that there was something missing. At that point, I crossed the room and picked up a huge white teddy bear. "This is the Higher Power," I explained, placing all the smaller bears in the white bear's huge embrace. "That is our ultimate protector. And we have all this inside us." In Chapter 11, we will further explore the connection with this Higher Power, or what I refer to as the Inner Self, and its role in the recovery of our Inner Child.

AWARENESS

With your dominant hand, write out your thoughts and feelings about the Protective Parent Within. Write about your experiences doing the exercises. Have you been able to bring your Protective Parent out in your life? Where and when? What happened?

Critical
Parent

SEVEN

Encountering Your Critical Parent

*Children have more need
of models than of critics.*

JOSEPH JOUBERT

Pensées

We all have a Critic residing in our mind. This voice broadcasts its messages—day or night, rain or shine—reminding us that we are not measuring up, not doing it right. We find this part of the psyche described in many schools of psychology. In Gestalt Therapy it is called the Top Dog. In Transactional Analysis it is the Critical Parent. In Voice Dialogue it is referred to simply as the Critic. I call this character the Critical Parent.

The Critical Parent loves to dominate and to be the boss. It always knows best. It likes to recite long lists of our faults, which it itemizes in detail. Very often when I interview the Critical Parent sub-personality in a therapy session, the individual takes on a decidedly parental air. It is not uncommon for the person who is speaking from the Critical Parent to stop in midsentence and say something like, "Oh, my God, this is my mother talking," or "Well, you just met my father." And it is true. When the Critic speaks I often see the person age before my very eyes. An older parent energy takes over, one that may bear little resemblance to the individual who came in for the session.

The Critical Parent wears many different faces and nicknames, depending on the person's family history. It may be a mother or father, a step-parent, uncle or aunt, or schoolteacher. Depending upon the cultural background, the Critical Parent may appear as Mother Superior, a Pig Parent, a Judge, an S.S. Trooper, a Sergeant. It may be male or female, but is usually an older, serious voice. Its function is to "straighten the individual out" through criticism.

The Critical Parent says things to us like: "You're a mess." "You're lazy." "What a jerk." "You'll never amount to anything." "You're so stupid." "What a fat slob." "Look at you, you're all skin and bones." "You've got to do something about your (skin, hair, legs, waistline, etc.)." The person's physical appearance is a favorite target of the Critical Parent, especially aspects of the body that cannot be changed. "The trouble with you is that you are male (or female), too tall (or too short), too young (or too old). You're not rich enough, smart enough, charming enough, or sophisticated enough." You get the idea. Give the Critical Parent an inch and it will take a mile.

The Critical Parent gets us to plastic surgeons and make-over demonstrations. Even if we try to please it, it finds something else to criticize. It is never satisfied. It loves to name-call, point out faults, pick on us. And it can be incredibly inventive in finding fault. The bottom line is that whatever we do, we are never good enough for the Critical Parent.

The Critical Parent Within develops at an early age. It learned from all those people in our early environment who criticized, blamed, and shamed us. Parents and other authority figures told us we were naughty, bad, a nuisance, messy, stupid, a "mistake" (especially if we were unwanted). These messages were reinforced year after year through repetition and constitute brainwashing. These negative statements that have been internalized are often called tapes. They have literally been recorded in the mind and encoded in the body. "You should be ashamed of yourself" often gets translated into slumping and postural misalignment. It certainly damages our self-esteem and distorts our belief system. When a child internalizes negative beliefs about itself, the Inner Critical Parent is in basic training. By adolescence this internalized Critical Parent goes into high gear, and by adulthood it holds forth in one's mind in quadraphonic sound.

A classic case of a Critical Parent run rampant is the following monologue done by a workshop participant. Notice that the Critical Parent attacks every area of her life.

> You're lazy . . . You don't dust . . . You don't vacuum . . . You hate to cook . . . You won't eat vegetables . . . You won't stay home You go to bed too late You eat cookies and chocolate in bed Your desk is cluttered Your refrig is dirty Your windows are dirty You don't sew on missing buttons You are a slob You don't take care of your bills until the last possible minute—This year you sent your xmas cards in Feb. You daydream—Then you rush around like mad You break dishes— You drop food— You spill on your best blouse— You don't answer your letters—you phone instead Your phone bill is too much. Your car is dirty You only water once a week You forget to turn off the sprinkler and the hose to soak a tree. Your shoes are all in a jumble in your closet. Your extra closet is full of clothes you got too fat to wear. You don't talk to your mother. You don't call your friend Marilyn Is she really your friend? She only gets in touch weith you when she needs something. George doesn't care about you—He won't call you or send you a birthday card or thank you for anything you give him.

If you feel exhausted after reading this litany of faults by someone else's Critical Parent, imagine how your own Inner Critic affects your energy level and health. In workshops, I sometimes ask people to read their Critical Parent put-downs out loud and to really dramatize them. Toward the end, members of the group are usually gasping for breath and sighing wearily. When it is over they are often howling with laughter. Some of them nervously share how painfully familiar that "voice" is. As one student put it: "They all sound like they went to the same night school for Critical Parenting." Others react with comments such as "That Critical Parent sounds so ridiculous when brought out into the open." They observe that its statements are out of proportion and out of touch with present reality. And that is precisely the point. To pull the covers off the Critical Parent is to expose it for what it is: an emperor with no clothes, a dictator with no power. It only has as much power as we give it.

One distinction that must be made here is that the Critical Parent is not to be confused with the voice of conscience. They are not the same. The Critical Parent attacks you for who you are. A truly healthy conscience asks us to look at our values and our behavior. Are we being true to ourself? Do our words match our actions? Are we "walking our talk?" A healthy conscience helps us to live an honest, self-reflective life. An uncontrolled Critical Parent makes life hell.

My first conscious awareness of the damage we do to children when we criticize and name-call happened when I was a young parent. My youngest daughter, Aleta, was a toddler at the time. It had been a difficult day, and I was stretched to the limit with two children under the age of three. Aleta had done something annoying and I reacted. "Aleta, you're a bad girl." I had never called her that before. Tears formed in her eyes and she responded passionately, "No, I'm not. I'm your SWEET girl!" I burst into tears, gathered her up in my arms, and said, "Yes, you are my sweet girl. I'm sorry, Aleta." I have never forgotten that moment, or the lesson I learned about how devastated a child feels when it is shamed for who it is. Pointing out unacceptable behavior is one thing, shaming a child's being is another.

Getting unhooked from our addiction to self-shaming (which we learned in childhood) means facing up to our Critical Parent Within. For this voice continues to make us feel shameful and bad, not only for what we do, but for who we are. It finds us inadequate to the core. We cannot DO anything to satisfy it. If we do not stop this destructive habit, we keep opening the wounds of childhood and there can be no healing, no recovery.

This is the big test in the hero's journey. This is where we face the dragon, confront the wicked witch, encounter the monster head-on. It is now that we see the "enemy" for what it is: our negative beliefs about ourselves, the attitude that we are bad, shameful, worthless. These beliefs came from outside. They were learned. They are not who we are. When we see them for what they are, we have a chance of liberating our Inner Child. (You can find additional techniques for changing your negative belief systems in my books *The Picture of Health: Healing Your Life With Art* and *The Well-Being Journal*.)

In the face of impossible standards in our family of origin, the Inner Child is crushed from the start. The more critical and demanding our caregivers were, the stronger hold our Inner Critical Parent will have on our lives. The same is true if we were neglected in childhood. Rather than recognizing inadequate parenting, the abandoned child usually concludes that there is something wrong with him or herself. This child develops as much self-blame and shame as one who was systematically judged and criticized. In both cases, the result is a relentless Inner Critical Parent and a devastated Inner Child.

We can see the damage done by a Critical Parent in the following letter from a woman's Inner Child. Writing with the non-dominant hand, the Vulnerable Child speaks of the hurt she still feels about the way her mother treated her. Her Inner Critical Parent was still treating her today the way her mother treated her in childhood.

Dear Mommy,

I doing the best I can. Why don't you like me? No matter what I do you don't like me. I try to please you and show things I do that I'm proud of, like the piano or my schoolwork, but you've always got to be first. Can't I be first sometime. I want you to be proud of me.

A good way to put the Critical Parent in perspective is to look it square in the face and let it talk. Usually it operates undercover, whispering away like background music. In this way it erodes our self-esteem. When we turn around to look at it directly, we have a chance to see it for what it is: just one part of the Inner Family. It is not the boss (even though some Critical Parents believe they are or should be).

In this chapter we will find out what the Critical Parent has to say for itself, through monologues and dialogues as well as pictures. We will start by writing a litany of all the self-critical messages your Critical Parent uses at this particular time in your life.

MEETING THE CRITICAL PARENT WITHIN

MATERIALS: Paper and felt pens.

With your non-dominant hand draw a picture of your Critical Parent.

THE Critical Parent

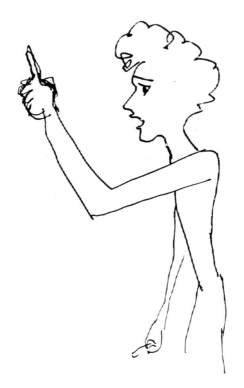

CRITICAL PARENT/ASSERTIVE CHILD

MATERIALS: Paper and felt pens. *Optional:* tape recorder and blank tape.

1. Look at the drawing of your Critical Parent.

2. With your dominant hand let the Critical Parent in your drawing talk. Write out what it says to you at this time in your life. Let the Critical Parent speak in the second person, as shown in the example:

Look at your desk. What a *mess*! How can you stand to live and work in such a pig sty? What a slob you are.

3. Read back (silently or aloud) the Critical Parent "speech." You might even want to tape-record it and play it back. If you read the "speech" aloud, really dramatize it. When you play it back let yourself really feel your reaction. It may sound ridiculously funny to you. It may make you angry. Whether you read it silently or aloud, experience whatever feelings spontaneously arise.

4. With your non-dominant hand, let your Inner Child write down its reaction to the Critical Parent. Stay true to your feelings about what the Critical Parent said.

The following dialogues were written by participants in one of my Inner Child workshops.

CRITICAL PARENT/ASSERTIVE CHILD

Parent: You are not together enough to do what you fantasize doing. For a smart person you're awfully dumb. You may think you're creative, but are you really? It takes you twice and maybe three times as long as other peers to complete things. You dawdle, day dream, alienate people who could help you. You really fritter away time and you isolate yourself. What makes you think you could have a productive life, make contribution, be creative. You are not together enough!

Child: I see you took up more room and left me less. I think you are trying to make me a helpless failure so you can have total control. I won't let you control me. I won't let you hold me back. You are a coward you are too afraid to risk and mess up. You can't do anything but undermine others. Leave me alone. Get out of my life and stay out!

CRITICAL PARENT/ASSERTIVE CHILD

Parent: You can't go out and play. Absolutely NOT!!! I beg your pardon. You want what? When your work is done, then and only then maybe I'll let you go outside. Now get to work clean your room, scrub the floor, clean up that mess. You're a slob. Get those clothes off the floor. What do you think this is? A party? You think you're here to play. NO SIR!! You're here to work! Your father and I have given you everything. Show your appreciation. Do what you're told. As long as you live in *this* house you'll do what I say. Jesus Christ Ida Lorraine, get your ass out of that chair and move it. After that your grandmother has sewing for you to do, then set the table for dinner. Maybe if you're good we'll go out later for an ice cream. Nothing less or else! When your father gets home you'll be in trouble unless you do what I say. And *no* outside until that homework is done. You are so lazy always waiting til the last minute. You've known about this report for three weeks.

Child: Fuck you asshole! I am here to play. I'm not your slave Do that work yourself if you want it done I'm going to go out right now and play and you can go fuck yourself Your jobs are not my responsibility. My father and you haven't given me shit Get off the fucking pedestal I don't even want to be living in this house You can take my homework and blow it out your ear Why would I give a fuck about homework when you and that bastard are killing me emotionally and physically I am going to do what I damn well please. I am going to play and indulge myself To hell with the homework and housework

CRITICAL PARENT/ASSERTIVE CHILD

Parent: I can't believe you—you don't do anything right. Here you are in this workshop & you couldn't even get the exercise right. And then there's your foot. What a baby! And I'm sure you're just limping around for attention. And if you weren't so fat you could get around much better. When are you gonna grow up! You just eat totally willfully! Don't you have any self control? And another thing, when are you going to go back to work and be productive? Everybody else managed to stay at work in spite of the stress, but not you. I've known for a long time that you are so weak and such a baby. All you have to do is just do it! It doesn't take any thought—just do it whatever it is. You just go into your feelings and wallow there and drown in them. It's no wonder you can't function. If you'd quit whining & feeling, grow up & get on with your life you'd be much better off. And by the way, you've done a lousy job with Matt. Just look at him—you've made a baby out of him too. He's not going to be able to function in the world with what you've done to him. And as far as other relationships—you don't even know how to have them. You pick lousy men & then you can't even get along with them—or with women friends for that matter. And then there's the matter of education. You're trying to get by with no education. You probably couldn't get a Masters anyway! You're so stupid!

Child: You know what—FUCK YOU! Who the hell are you to talk to me like that! I'm not lazy & I am smart! You make me feel like crying when you say those things to me. Why don't you leave me alone! Get lost! All you ever do is yell at me—so go fuck yourself! STOP! STOP! STOP! STOP!

STOP!

Leave me alone. I don't want you around me. All you do is make me feel bad.

The litany of faults recited by the Critical Parent usually contains clear statements that reveal our negative beliefs about ourselves. In reprogramming our destructive belief systems, we can start with these monologues of the Critical Parent. Affirmation techniques can then be used. Earlier I mentioned two of my other books, as they contain simple guidelines on how to identify and change self-defeating beliefs.

One area of our lives where it is essential that we deal with the Critical Parent is in facing creative blocks. The enemy of creative expression is the Critical Parent. If allowed to run rampant, it paralyzes us. In demanding excellence and perfection at all times, the Critical Parent robs the Inner Child of the experimentation phase that is the essential first step in the creative process.

Creative blocks can include fear of change, writer's or artist's block, or chronic low energy. Such blocks are symptoms that the Creative Child has fallen under the spell of a Critical Parent Within. The Child wants to speak. If it cannot express its feelings, it will not be able to express creativity either.

You may be experiencing a block in your life at this time. Is there *something you really want to do* but cannot seem to do? If so, this may be just the technique to help you break through to the other side—and achieve your heart's desire.

HEART'S DESIRE

MATERIALS: Paper and felt pens.

1. With your dominant hand, ask your Inner Child to tell you its heart's desire—something it has always wanted to do or be. Often this is something buried deep inside because the Child was afraid (and rightfully so) of being put down by the Critical Parent. Let your Child write out its heart's desire with the non-dominant hand.

2. Now, writing with your dominant hand, let the Critical Parent state its opinions about the Inner Child's heart's desire. Then, encourage your Inner Child to answer back with your non-dominant hand. Allow your Inner Child to assert itself and express how it *really* feels. Remember, this is a safe place to let the Child express.

3. Now ask your Inner Child to draw a picture of itself after achieving its heart's desire. Put the picture up where you can look at it frequently. Get into the habit of visualizing it in your mind's eye. Use it as a visual affirmation of your Child's heart's desire.

4. With your dominant hand, write down the steps you will take to help your Inner Child achieve its heart's desire. Write these steps out in your calendar or day planner to ensure that you honor your commitment. If blocks recur, repeat the exercise.

Criticism From Others

As we become more conscious of the Critical Parent Within, we may start noticing this voice in other people around us. The Critical Parent voice will be especially evident in authority figures and those who we feel have "power" over us. They may have jobs or positions in society that are associated with authority: judges, police, teachers, doctors, and clergy. Or they may play a more personal role in our lives: parents, landlords, or employers. We may even confer the status of authority figure on our mate, older siblings, or certain friends.

Regardless of their place in society, anyone who can belittle or intimidate us is functioning as a Critical Parent, an authority figure (whether it is intentional or not). If we are unaware of how our Inner Critical Parent nags us mercilessly, it is easy to project it onto others. We see all the criticism coming from the outside and we react to it as if it is *their* fault, *them doing it to us*. In this scenario, we become the poor innocent victim, while *they* (critical and abusive people) become the bad guys.

The way out of this dilemma is to take responsibility for our part in this little drama. As Eleanor Roosevelt once said, "Nobody can do anything to me that I am not already doing to myself." No one gets away with destructive criticism unless we consent to it. Our Protective Parent can refuse to permit criticism that damages our Child's self-esteem.

Without a good honest look at our own self-criticism, it is easy to continue projecting it onto others. The problem needs to be addressed at its roots: inside. We do this by recognizing our own Critical Parent Within and dealing with it ourselves.

The following activity enables you to pinpoint the people in your life who you experience as authority figures. If they are critical and judgmental of you, you will let them speak. However, you will also let your Protective Parent respond on paper. Since the other person is not present, your Child is safe. The Protective Parent can say anything it wishes. There is no need to be polite or respectful. There is no reason to rescue or obey this critical voice.

STANDING UP FOR YOUR INNER CHILD

MATERIALS: Paper and felt pens.

1. Think about someone in your life who intimidates or belittles you. If there are more than one, just focus on one in particular right now.

2. With your non-dominant hand draw a picture of this person belittling or intimidating you. In your drawing include word bubbles (like the ones shown in cartoons). What does the intimidator say? How do you feel? Write your feelings into a thought bubble next to yourself in the picture.

3. Continue portraying the interaction in your picture by writing out a dialogue between your Protective Parent and the other person. Let your Protective Parent write with your dominant hand. The other person's voice will also speak through your dominant hand. Remember, you can say whatever you feel: the other person is not standing in front of you physically.

    Note: It is crucial that you keep this work private. If you are afraid that someone will read it without permission, it will be very difficult to be honest about your feelings. Without honest expression, this exercise yields little or no benefit. Protect your right to privacy in whatever way you choose.

4. With your non-dominant hand, redraw the picture of yourself and the other person. Let this drawing show *the way you would like to feel* in the situation or in the relationship.

5. Optional: If you need to strengthen your Protective Parent in dealing with the person in these dialogues, go back to Chapter 6 and apply the exercises entitled, "Drawing Out Your Protective Parent" and "Protective Parent: Role-Playing."

AWARENESS

With your dominant hand, write down your experience of your own Critical Parent Within. How does it affect your life? What have you learned about how to deal with it? Review the work you did in this chapter. Write down your reactions. In what areas of your life do you feel blocked by your Critical Parent?

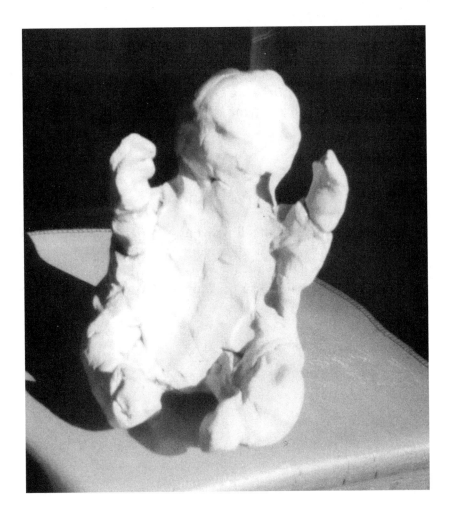

BROKEN CHILD

Sister/Brother
Broken child
Cut asunder
in the wild

Separated . . .
Lost from sight
This voice was muffled
in the night

(Poem and clay sculpture of Inner Child by workshop participant.)

182

EIGHT

Healing the Wounds of Childhood

I wonder if there's enough paper in the world to hold what I need to say. I've been silent for so long!!!

—JANEL TEMPLE
Incest Survivor

One of the most gratifying aspects of my work is witnessing the growth of people who are healing themselves. The following letter from an incest survivor will give you a glimpse of a woman finding her true voice after being "silent for so long."

Dear Ms. Capacchione:

I wish I could share with you the progression of my journaling process since I discovered your book, THE CREATIVE JOURNAL. I began remembering the severe sexual and physical abuse of my childhood about 9 months ago. My journal from February through May is a stack of lined notebook paper with black and blue words on it. (How appropriate!) May 22 is my first entry on unlined paper—fantastic scribbles. My most recent "entry" is on a piece of 27" x 34" news-print—I call it "My Inner Self—in Celebration of the Children". It's done in big, beautiful bold colors.

Your book has enabled me to touch parts of myself that I never knew existed, because they've been numb so long.

I was always (or at least always felt like) a person who should stay away from "art" because I was no good at it. If anyone tried to teach me about self-expression, I don't remember it. It was probably too dangerous when I was a child anyway.

I can't wait to show this most recent piece of work (crayola marker on newsprint?!) to my therapist. It's delightful—and I have you to thank for opening up the possibilities.

The newsprint seems small now—sometimes I wonder if there's enough paper in the world to hold what I need to say. I've been silent for so long!!!

I'm one of those responsible people who always types business letters. I wrote this for my journal, but my journey is too big now to keep it internal and secret. So I'm defying the straight lines and rules and sending it to you with a world full of thank you's for having the courage and caring to publish your book. You have helped me connect with myself.

Thank you. Sincerely,
Janel Temple

I chose to introduce this chapter on Healing the Wounds of Childhood with this letter because it shares the experience, strength and hope of an incest survivor. Of all the forms of wounding in childhood, this is probably the most heartbreaking. And yet, when such a survivor re-parents that wounded Child Within, it ultimately empowers all of us. These people are truly heroes and heroines of our time.

More desperately than ever, we need to hear such inspirational stories. We need hope in the face of widespread child abuse in our society. The newspapers and media are filled with reports of child abuse perpetrated by adults charged with care of the young. The most notable example is the McMartin pre-school case in California, in which the school's owners, a mother and son, were charged with multiple counts of child abuse. This case was the longest, most costly trial in U.S. history. We also see reports of parents (like Charles Rothenberg) who maim and disfigure their own children. We need some success stories to counteract this dreadful trend. For this reason those adult survivors of child abuse who are willing to speak out are providing badly needed leadership in turning the tide on child abuse. Abuse thrives on secrecy. Once the secret is out there is hope for healing and recovery.

Traditionally, psychotherapy has addressed itself to early trauma—the wounds of childhood. From the beginning of modern psychological theory and treatment it was agreed that unresolved childhood experiences reverberate throughout our lives. Like a stone dropped in a pond sending ripples out to the far shore, the impact of early painful events long outlives the moment. Theories about healing these childhood traumas have come in different packages—Freudian, Jungian, Adlerian, and so on—but the theme has always been there. Over time, therapeutic techniques have varied—from talking about childhood memories, to writing or telling personal histories, to regression into the Child state. Regardless of the method, the goal has been the same: healing the wounds of childhood.

In recent times, the acknowledgment of widespread child abuse has made us more aware than ever of the need for safe settings and techniques for healing the Child Within. For abused children grow into adults, but the hurt, Vulnerable Child Within does not grow up. It is this unhealed aspect of childhood—as it lives on in the adult—that we will explore now. You may have already encountered residues of painful childhood experiences while doing the previous exercises. These leftover feelings and memories may have seeped through in some of the dialogues with your Inner Child.

In this chapter, we focus on healing our past by becoming a counselor to that hurt Child still living within us. By giving the Child *today* the attention and acceptance it needed long ago, by showing it *now* the understanding and compassion it wanted then, we begin to heal the old wounds. You may or may not consider yourself a victim of child abuse. I am assuming that if you are reading this book and doing the exercises you have *some* Inner Child healing to do. Let's face it, we all had painful experiences of one kind or another in childhood. If those are unresolved, these exercises can be extremely beneficial.

Where It All Begins

Often we think of a child's life beginning at birth. As for earliest *conscious* memories, those usually begin much later—depending upon the individual. Some people's first memories take them back to age two or before. Other people cannot recall anything before they were three, four, or five years old. However, with certain techniques, some individuals actually remember intrauterine experience or their birth.

For instance, one of my clients, Gloria, drew her feelings in an art therapy session. As she expressed her feelings of emptiness and abandonment, she began to cry. Without realizing it, she had drawn a fetus. "I wasn't wanted," she said tearfully. "I just felt it right now. When my mother was pregnant with me, she didn't want another baby. Neither of them did." She went on to explain that her parents had never actually told her this, but that when she saw the fetus in her drawing she knew. It wasn't intellectual, it was gut knowing. She did know that her birth had been long and difficult. She concluded by reflecting: "I've always been soft-spoken and shy. I think I've spent my whole life trying not to be here, trying to fade into the background so I wouldn't upset my parents, who didn't want me in the first place." Then she smiled and said, "I guess *I have to want me* and decide whether to be here or not—I mean *really be here.*" Fortunately, Gloria did choose to *be here.* She eventually became an artist, a risk she had never been willing to take before. As she put it, "For me, displaying my art means I am making a statement. I am saying, 'See, here I am. I do exist and I want you to notice me.' "

Sometimes in written dialogues with the Inner Child (such as the ones included in the previous chapters), an individual will actually regress to the birth experience. If the birth was a difficult one, the healing that comes about is quite profound. The following drawing and dialogue were done by a man who attended one of my Inner Child workshops. When he shared his rebirth process, the group was visibly moved by what he read to us. I had assigned an Inner Child drawing and dialogue. This man began by drawing a baby under a tree. He then went on to have a right/left-hand dialogue with the baby, who turned out to be his newborn infant self.

Adult: How old are you?

Child: A few weeks.

Adult: How do you feel?

Child: Sick, tiny, struggling, afraid, fighting for my life.

Adult: Why?

Child: I'm a preemy—3lbs at most. Had a mid-wife for delivery . . . . not supposed to live.

Adult: Where are you?

Child: At my Grandmothers in Miss.

Adult: Where's your mother?

Child: I don't know.

Adult: Tell me about your Grandmother.

Child: She wants me to live . . . Dr. Furr . . . is helping. . . . I want to live too. But most think I won't . . . I'll show them! I'll get out of this shoe box with a pillow.

Adult: What are you going to do now?

Child: Scream & cry so my lungs will grow—They think I'm hungry but I'm mad and determined!

Adult: What else?

Child: Being little sucks. I want to grow up.

Adult: What makes you feel good?

Child: The sound of the Kakadia dids in the evening and the smell of the water in the Coldwater River that goes in front of my Aunt Lillie's house. Nature is my mother and my father! I can trust nature.

Adult: Who do you distrust?

Child: Grownups—parents will let you down like mine have. See, they're not here to see me live or die.

Adult: Your Grandmother?

Child: I'll live for her. We love each other.

You can heal painful associations you have surrounding your birth by letting your Inner Child speak. This pain may come from the awareness that your parents did not want a child when you were conceived (as in the case of Gloria). It may also come from being told that your parents wanted a child of the opposite sex, or one who looked different than you do.

In the next exercise you will explore your attitudes about your birth and re-create the experience the way you would have wanted it to be.

MY BIRTH

MATERIALS: Paper and felt pens.

1. Have a dialogue with your Inner Child. With your non-dominant hand let your Child write about your birth. What did it hear from others about your birth? Does it have any memories of its own? How does it feel about your birth?

2. With your dominant hand explain to your Inner Child that you want to give it the kind of birth that it wants and deserves. Ask the Child to tell you exactly what kind of birth it wants. Let the Child describe its birth with your non-dominant hand in the present tense. Follow this with a drawing of the new birth described by your Inner Child.

Becoming Your Own Counselor

Childhood can be extremely lonely, especially if parents and caregivers do not understand children, or are unable to listen. As we were growing up there were so many feelings, so many experiences we just could not talk about. But the Inner Child can talk about them now. And we can be there to listen.

In the next series of exercises, you will travel back in time and be there with the Child you once were. As a counselor to your Inner Child of the past, you can now offer yourself the comfort and love you were denied in childhood.

COUNSELING YOUR CHILD OF THE PAST

MATERIALS: Crayons, pastels, felt pens, and paper.

1. With the non-dominant hand draw a time in your childhood when you felt hurt, sad, or abandoned and had no one there to comfort you.

2. With your dominant hand, explain that you are here now and want to let the Child feel its feelings and share them safely with you. Ask the Inner Child to write down (with the non-dominant hand) what happened and how it felt.

3. Ask the Inner Child if there is anything it wants in order to feel better. Ask it to draw you a picture of itself feeling safe, comforted, and loved.

4. Then ask your Inner Child to write (with the non-dominant hand) anything else it wants to tell you.

From time to time repeat this exercise, concentrating on a different childhood experience each time. If you are unsure of which experience to use as your focus, try working with feelings that are coming up in your life at this time. For instance, if a current situation triggers feelings of abandonment, do this exercise. Go back in time to an early experience of abandonment. Picture it on paper with your non-dominant hand and do a written dialogue as previously described. Here is a list of feelings that you can explore with your Inner Child of the Past:

Frightened	Overwhelmed
Sad	Exhausted
Grieving	Despondent
Lonely	Hopeless
Hurt (emotionally or physically)	Lost
Abandoned	Confused
Sick	Angry
Abused	Shy

In the following drawings and writings done by some of my readers and workshop participants, the Inner Child of the Past tells about its fears, its anger, and its sadness.

Beware of dog

"Stay away from this big dog with the purple tongue. If he bites you, it will make you die! My brother told me that. I never went near him. I walked all the way around the block to go to school so the dog wouldn't get me. I told my Mother. She bought us a dog to keep in the house!! I made them keep him under the cellar stairs because I never went down there. His name was Toby and he was black. One

day my Mother made me go down
those long dark stairs to see him. I
didn't want him to bite me and make me
die. She forced me. I peeked under the
stairs and all I could see was a big
pile of black fuzz. He jumped up and
licked me. "I'm dead now!" But I wasn't!
I looked at his tongue. I wasn't purple. It
was pink just like mine. He liked me so
I just liked him back. He was my best
friend. He waited for me to come home.
He stuck his head out
of the railing on the
porch and waited for me

People used to mess around with my hair

they used to tie my
hair all up in rags and
make me sleep on the
knots. Boy did that
hurt.

My Grama used to wring
my hair out like the wash.
I said "Grama that hurts me"
but she did it anyway.
"Ouch! Ouch"

One time a real barber cut
my hair. It was awful. My ears
stuck out and I looked like
a boy. I wore a hat for
a long time.

This didn't turn out like on
the t.v. where they said "which
Twin has the Toni?" They lied.
I looked like a big ball of
steel wool.

This is what happened to me in Kindergarten.

Mrs. carpel was my teacher.

I was really little and skinny and afraid. my socks used to fall down.

you are so stupid and clumsy. you are a retarded little girl!

pots of
paint

i loved painting. it was the best most
wonderful thing. i painted my visions +
my house, family. I loved all the colors
and i loved painting a happy world of
my own on paper.
Mrs. Carpel got very very mad at
me because on several conseortive
days i spilled the cans of paint.
She yelled at me + told me i was
stupid + clumsy. She told my
mother i was mentally retarded
and wanted her to switch me to an
M.R. class.

after that i was even more
afraid. i cried more. and i
was afraid of flunking tests.
i did very poorly in school.
i was nearsighted but no one
knew because i memorized the
eye charts + fooled the school
nurse.

there was a lot of yelling at
my house. Daddy yelled a lot.
i felt afraid + i used to hide
in my closet with a pillow + blanket.

yes thats
right.

E

right side

195

When Robert did a dialogue with his Child of the Past, a very frightened little boy emerged. Although very tall as an adult, in childhood Robert was small and surrounded by older brothers and sisters and their friends. He was called names and teased. By the end of the dialogue, Little Robert was able to assert himself in words and in a picture.

When people read these dialogues out loud in workshops, the group always applauds the Inner Child who "tells it like it is." It is a victory for everyone. The following is Robert's dialogue and drawing.

Adult: Who are you?

Child: Your Inner Child.

Adult: How do you feel?

Child: Scared. I'm so scared of big people. I'm so small and no one pays any attention to me. Its too much. I can't take it.

Adult: Why do you feel this way?

Child: Big people hurt me and make fun of me.

Adult: What can I do to help you?

Child: Be strong. Protect me.

Adult: What's your name?

Child: Shrimpy.

Adult: Who gave you that name?

Child: My sister.

Adult: Do you like her?

Child: No she is mean.

Adult: What does she do to you?

Child: She says mean things, lies to Mom and hits me.

Adult: Do you like your brother?

Child: He's ok. But he picks on me & beats me up. He's so big.

Adult: Would you like to say something to your sister?

Child: Leave me alone!

Adult: Would you like to say something to your brother?

Child: Quit picking on me!

I used to be very very sad when big people yelled at me. I always seemed to do all the wrong things and people would get mad at me or even worse they would laugh at me. Then they told me I was stupid or fat or ugly. Sometimes it hurt my little body and mind so much that I would hide under the table and just stay out of everybody's way. - boo-hoo

Everything was going pretty good until my father came home one day when I was seven and said we were moving away from our house in Hamilton. I didn't understand until one day the house was all empty and so was I. We got in the car and drove away. I cried and cried. I had to leave all my friends, my school, my bedroom — everything was left behind. I didn't even know where we were going or why we had to leave. I'll come back some day!!!

Sadness from childhood can stay with us for a lifetime if it is not openly acknowledged. In doing what is called "grief work," we allow the Inner Child of the Past to express its hidden sadness, to feel it, and to be understood. In the Inner Child writings and drawings on pages 198 and 199, early experiences of sadness are revisited through illustrated storytelling.

The Grieving Process

An important part of Inner Child healing is the grieving process. I say "process" because it takes time and it takes strength to face one's buried grief. For instance, some adult survivors of child abuse come to the realization one day that they never really had a childhood. They discover that they were "parentalized children" and were forced to be little grown-ups from an early age. Sarah was the oldest of several children. Her father, an alcoholic, was never around. When he did come home, he was in a drunken stupor. Her mother was chronically overwhelmed, worried. The job of mother's helper fell upon Sarah's shoulders from as early as she can remember (probably from age two, when her brother was born). She cannot recall ever playing with classmates or neighborhood children. Her childhood consisted of school, homework, housework, and baby-sitting.

When Sarah could finally talk about it, she admitted that she felt cheated. Something had been taken away from her. The fact is that she was robbed of her *child*hood. Eventually she developed the strength to express her deep sorrow. As she did this in the context of re-parenting herself, she discovered SaSa, an adorable Inner Child. She certainly had lots of experience with children, so when she began caring for SaSa, she did a wonderful job. Paradoxically, it was through the grieving process that she developed the strength to lovingly parent her Inner Child.

When we grieve over anyone's death, it is the Inner Child who grieves. If we block the process and do not allow it to unfold naturally, we end up holding on to the pain. It's like getting a lump in your throat when you forbid yourself to cry. Unexpressed grief can damage us emotionally and physically. Studies have shown that many people are diagnosed with cancer about a year or so after the death of a loved one. I have also seen this pattern in people who have recently retired.

When we grieve, the Vulnerable Child needs to feel. It may be angry and want to shout. It may need to cry, to be held, to be treated with great tenderness. It is our Nurturing Parent who can offer that tender, loving self-care in those moments of heartbreaking sorrow and aloneness.

The most moving portrayal of this process I have ever seen was in the television special *Nobody's Child,* directed by Lee Grant and starring Marlo Thomas. It is a true story about an adult survivor of extreme child abuse who spent many years in mental institutions. She was considered hopeless until she eventually received help from a hospital staff member who believed in her. As the story unfolds, we see this courageous survivor build a new life. She is released from the institution and later marries. But the story is not over yet. Later on, when her husband dies, we see the woman in a poignant and unforgettable scene. Alone at home after the funeral, she sees an image of herself as a child. Through special effects, we see her holding and comforting a young girl—her child of the Past—who slowly dissolves in to her. She is able to grieve over her husband's death because she has developed a healthy relationship with her Inner Child. This woman went on to dedicate herself to helping others, and eventually a mental institution was named after her. When I think of heroic survivors of child abuse, I always remember *Nobody's Child.*

Many years ago, I had a deeply transforming experience with the grief process. I had gone to my favorite spiritual retreat center for a quiet weekend of introspection. There were no programs to attend, no demands to meet, only a time of quiet personal renewal. In between walks through the gardens and periods of silence in a special meditation chapel nestled off among the trees, I did journal work in my room. From a desk at my window on the second floor I could look out over the treetops, watching the clouds drift past and the birds fly about. In this beautiful and safe place, I drew and wrote dialogues with my Inner Child.

A young girl came out on the pages of my journal. She told me of buried grief over the death of a loved one that had occurred many years before.

This was a surprise, for I thought I had already grieved over my loss. I had cried. I had felt sadness. Wasn't that enough? But, no, this tender young girl inside me was still grieving. She needed this quiet time and place to feel safe enough to come out and grieve some more. She needed a kind of solitude she had not had at the time of the death. There had always been family and professional responsibilities in the way. So I gave her the wholehearted attention of my Nurturing Parent, and the healing that resulted was profound. I sobbed and sobbed for hours. It was painful, but it was worth every tear, for it felt like a spring rain clearing away the dead past. It was an unforgettable weekend and stands out as a major healing experience.

SAYING GOOD-BYE

As you do some of the activities in this book, you may stumble across sorrow over the loss of people, pets, or things that meant a lot to you. Let the Child talk about its feelings with your non-dominant hand. Let the tears come. With your dominant hand offer reassurance that it is okay for the Child to feel sad and to cry.

If you are finding it difficult to nurture your Inner Child, it might help to remember someone in your childhood with whom you felt safe and loved. Here's an exercise to assist you in recalling such a person.

A NURTURING PERSON FROM CHILDHOOD

MATERIALS: Paper and felt pens.

1. Think about some nurturing people from your childhood. How did they show their love and affection? Focus on one of these nurturing people.

2. With your non-dominant hand, write about a time in childhood when you felt nurtured. Describe a time when you were a youngster that this person offered care and friendship.

3. If there is something troubling you at this time in your life, write a dialogue with that Nurturing Person from the Past. Using the non-dominant hand, tell the person about your problem. With your dominant hand let the Nurturing Person respond.

Once, during a particularly challenging period in my life, a powerful image came to me in meditation. I was in much confusion about my career direction and sources of income. Needing comfort and reassurance that things would be okay, I cleared my mind and waited for guidance. Suddenly I reexperienced what it was like sitting on my Grandma Lucia's lap as a small child. Drifting back to those early years, I felt totally loved, nurtured, and protected from all harm by her warm embrace. In the meditation she was huge—much larger than life. She said, ''Don't worry, I'm much bigger than you are. I can see much further ahead. I can see way into the future, and everything looks wonderful. You will be fine.''

Upon coming out of that meditation, a feeling of peace and contentment enveloped me. I realized then that my grandmother's love, which had been a real experience in childhood, was still with me. My memory of being loved for myself was something that could never be taken away from me. What a precious gift she had given me. I have called upon her many times since then, and she has always consoled my Inner Child.

Visual art can be an important reinforcement for a new attitude of self-nurturing. If there is a time in childhood that needs healing, embodying it in three-dimensional sculpture can help you really feel self-nurturing.

TENDER, LOVING CARE

MATERIALS: Clay, work surface (such as masonite, wood, or a plastic drop cloth), clean-up supplies, and appropriate work area, e.g., kitchen, garage, outdoors.

1. Make a sculpture of your Inner Parent caring for your Vulnerable Child of the Past.

2. Display the sculpture in a place where you can see it frequently.

Healing the Inner Child of the Past includes celebrating the happy times as well as the painful ones. Focusing on trauma to the exclusion of happy experiences keeps us out of balance, looking at the world through gray-colored glasses. If we do not appreciate our happy times with gratitude, we rob ourselves of vast inner resources. Our ability to make ourselves happy is a skill we need to practice. Here is a reminder.

HAPPY TIMES

MATERIALS: Crayons, pastels, felt pens, and paper.

Ask your Inner Child of the Past if there was a time in your childhood when it was happy. Invite the Child to share that time with you now by drawing or writing about it with your non-dominant hand.

LETTERS TO YOUR PARENTS OR CAREGIVERS

1. With your non-dominant hand, let your Inner Child write a letter to a parent or caregiver from childhood. From the new perspective you have gained about yourself while doing the exercises in this book, let your Inner Child say anything it wants in your letter.

2. If it feels right, let your Inner Child write a letter of forgiveness to a parent or caregiver with your non-dominant hand. This letter is not to be sent, but is intended for your own healing. It must be genuine. If you do not feel forgiveness, do not force this letter. Let it happen in its own time.

The following poem was written by the same woman who wrote "Broken Child" (at the beginning of this chapter). This later poem entitled "Mine," shows that much healing has taken place.

MINE

I am little you see
Hardly grown-up at all
I come from the depths
And fear I'll still fall.

My bruises are deep
But now healing begins
There's a path I must seek
And I know that I'll win.

With bowers of flowers
And birds for just me
And smiles and compassion
For the babe who's set free

And warm willing hands
That uplift me when down
That touch and don't hurt
The child with eyes brown.

I now can peek out
From my cold withdrawn place
And lift my eyes up
With true smiles on my face.

The future is mine
Past pain disappears
The sad wounded child
No longer has tears.

There's a glint in her eyes
And strength in her spine
I have one life to lead
And that life is now mine.

AWARENESS

With your dominant hand, write down your feelings about what you read in this chapter. What was your reaction to the sharing of other people's healing process? What happened for you as you did the exercises?

PART III

Giving Birth to the Magical Child

This last phase of re-parenting is like dessert. It is the reunion with that unlimited joy and creativity that the healed Inner Child offers us. The Child's gifts are: playfulness, wonderment, spontaneity, and just plain fun. The Inner Child provides the magic for those who are young at heart, regardless of their chronological age. The Inner Child who feels safe and protected, loved and nurtured, has an open heart and an open mind. It is free to love and be loved.

The aspects of ourselves that we will be exploring now are the Playful, Creative, and Spiritual Child. They are all closely connected, yet show us different facets of the same spirit. Each of these Inner Children has its own needs and its own unique contribution to make to our lives. In recent years these aspects of the Inner Child have been referred to as the Magical Child, the Playful Child, and the Precious Child. This is the child whose essence is love, the Holy Infant, the Child of God.

In their book *Embracing Our Selves*, Stone and Winkelman write:

The discovery of the inner child is really the discovery of a portal to the soul. A spirituality that is not grounded in understanding, experience, and an appreciation of the inner child can move people away from their simple humanity too easily. The inner child keeps us human. It never grows up, it only becomes more sensitive and trusting as we learn how to give it the time, care, and parenting it so richly deserves.

The paradox is that the more the Inner Child reveals itself to us, the more deeply we connect with the wisest, most ancient and eternal part of ourselves. The spirit of the little child leads us to our divine essence, the God within. This has been referred to as the Higher Power or the Higher Self. I call it the *Inner Self.*

You're so beautiful... what's your name? How old are you? I'm ROSIE, I'm TEN! Love me. Don't I do that now? How do you want me to love you? You put me away too long. Love me. Play with me. Take me out. Let me talk. I'm listening. Play. Play. Play. Water. Wind. Sun. Air. Outside. Take me out. Don't take you out. Take me out !

NINE

Letting Your Child Out to Play

Maturity means reacquiring
the seriousness one had
as a child at play.

—NIETZSCHE

The film *Harold and Maude* is a modern fairy tale about the archetypal Inner Child. Harold is Everychild, in that he is not understood by his parents. A poor little rich boy, Harold is the son of a narcissistic, controlling, critical mother. She is totally out of touch with the needs of her teenage son. In a desperate attempt to make some sort of contact with his mother, Harold spends his time staging gory mock suicides. Her response is to become increasingly exasperated and critical. She does not get the message that her son is crying out for love and attention.

Harold's mother resembles the step-mother in Disney's *Snow White*: haughty, vain and heartless. She wants to get rid of him, for him to grow up and get married. She tries to match him up with young women of *her* choice. Playing out the archetype of the domineering Critical Parent, she is obsessed with appearances, status, and societal approval. Again, Harold is Everychild, because (like all of us) he wants to be seen, heard, and accepted for who he is, not for what his mother wants him to be.

Harold and Maude is a modern-day version of the traditional tale of the lost or abandoned child (Cinderella, Hansel and Gretel, Snow White). Like these child heroes, Harold is caught in the grip of a powerful, unfeeling "witch." And true to the patterns of many myths and fairy tales, Harold finds a magical helper, a fairy godmother, in the person of Maude.

Maude embodies the paradox of healing. By society's standards, she is an old woman with no status, no material wealth. Certainly, she is not glamorous like Harold's mother. Yet Maude is beautiful to the core, because her Inner Child is alive and kicking. She sparkles, because she loves life, embraces it, and dances through her days. Naturally, Harold falls in love with her (to his family's great dismay). Actually, he is falling in love with the Inner Child archetype that she expresses so strongly, as well as the Nurturing Parent aspect of Maude. She shows him how to honor the Child within himself who had been denied by his own mother. By setting the example, Maude teaches Harold acceptance of himself as he is. She is many things to Harold: parent, playmate, mentor, and finally lover. But when the time is ripe she lets him go. She dies, consciously, admonishing him to go and love more, *to own the love he feels for her and to spread it around.* By dying she demonstrates another paradox: she helps him find his own joy in life. Instead of projecting his Inner Child or Inner Parent onto Maude and becoming dependent upon her, Harold must now find the Child and Parent in himself. *Harold and Maude* can be a profoundly healing movie for one who is on the hero's journey of healing the Inner Child. The character of Maude is a delightful portrait of the Playful and Creative Child in action.

The Playful Child in us has the capacity for real joy. I am not talking about the substitutes adults and teenagers call fun, such as getting "high" on alcohol or drugs, etc. Nor am I suggesting that we should act in a childish manner, pretending to be childlike. No, the Playful Child is the natural child who is capable of being truly joyful, like a little baby who delights in being alive. Our Playful Child enjoys simple pleasures: running on a beach, playing with a pet, hiking in the woods, hanging out with a favorite pal, eating a juicy piece of fruit with our hands, playing games, or even singing in the shower.

If you have difficulty finding your Playful Child, visit a children's park or playground. Just observe kids at play. Playfulness is as natural to healthy children as breathing. They do it all the time. They find any excuse to play or turn an activity into fun. In observing children, notice what kinds of things they seem to enjoy. Notice how they express joy through facial expressions, sounds, body language, and words.

In Chapter 5, you read Sue's account of how she healed her pain at not having her own children. She worked with children, videotaped and drew them. In one of her beautifully illustrated letters, Sue described a lovely experience she had while freeze-framing portions of her video:

> I found many wonderful shots—a little girl comes to mind who literally danced her way down the street in a red and white dress and huge sombrero type hat. When I froze her motion, I captured a look of joy that I had never seen before. It was something akin to the mystical and my response to it was to watch it again and again. The more of these children I watched, the more my inner heart was filled with joy and healing.

If we want to know how to play, we can just ask the Playful Child. It is our best teacher. In a workshop George asked his Playful Child what it wanted to do in his life. This is what the Child asked for:

> music & movement, to walk at the ocean, see the dawn, walk in the woods, gather treasures, play in the sand and mud, paint, swim, fly, and learn to scuba dive, get hugs.

The Playful Child is often active physically, as was George's, and has a strong influence on our health and vitality. Without the presence of an active Playful Child Within, exercise regimes (done out of a sense of duty) usually become boring and tedious. I believe that any form of exercise that does not engage our Playful Child is ultimately doomed. We rebel against it, and rightly so. Our bodies were meant to be enjoyed.

Watching an adult's Playful Child emerge is such a delightful experience. The person seems to grow younger before your very eyes. Elizabeth attended a two-day Inner Child workshop in order to liberate her playful self. On the second day of the workshop, she wore new running shoes and was quite proud of them. It was obvious that her Playful Child was out. In a drawing activity, she created a lively portrait of her own Playful Child, full of life and energy. Then, in a dialogue, Elizabeth found out what her Playful Child liked to do. It is really quite simple. After she shared her dialogue, people commented that she looked more youthful than the day before.

Elizabeth's drawing and dialogue with her Playful Child follow. Notice the humor, play on words, and poetic language.

Adult: Who are you?

Child: A dancer

Adult: How old are you?

Child: I'm ten

Adult: What is your name?

Child: Airee

Adult: What do you like to do?

Child: run bearfoot in grass

Adult: What else do you like to do?

Child: play tricks

Adult: on who?

Child: Mom—Dad, Evelyn

Adult: Is it fun to do that?

Child: Yes they're cerious
(like cerious clouds)
that was a trick on you

Adult: Oh I get it—tricks are jokes.

Child: Yes life is funny very funny

Adult: How do you feel today?

Child: Welp. Kinda stiff

Adult: How come?

Child: No big movement I want to but now I'm stiff like I forgot how to run without hurting myself or steepping on a rock twisting my foot

Adult: Is there anything else you'd like me to know about you?

Child: the new shoes are for me! I am happy but crackely on the edges and like frosted glass.

Adult: Thank you.

DRAWING OUT YOUR PLAYFUL CHILD

MATERIALS: Crayons, felt pens, pastels, and paper.

1. With your non-dominant hand let your Playful Child draw a picture of itself playing. Put word balloons in the picture and let your Playful Child tell what it likes to do for fun.

2. Have a written dialogue with your Playful Child. With your non-dominant hand ask the Child how it wants to play in your life at this time. Find out what areas of your life it feels left out of. Is the Child welcome in your relationships, sports, hobbies, etc.? Ask it which people in your life it feels O.K. with and which it feels excluded from. Your Playful Child responds with the non-dominant hand.

3. Ask your Playful Child to draw pictures (with your non-dominant hand) of the things it wants to do in your life right now. Let the Child write captions or sentences under the pictures, using the present tense, e.g., "I am running on the beach at sunset, watching the pretty colors of the sky and feeling the squishy wet sand under my feet. I'm free as the wind."

4. Display these pictures where you can look at them frequently. Use them as visual and verbal affirmations, reminders of your Playful Child's needs and wants.

In a workshop, Kathleen dialogued with her Playful Child, who also did some whimsical illustrations.

Adult: What is your name?

Child: I am Katy.

Adult: How do you feel about being here, Katy?

Child: I happy I get to come out! I wanted to come all week I'm excited! I love to ride around and see things like mountains and oceans and I love to be outside I wrote my name down to come here in January. I want us to go more and see everything.

Adult: What do you want from this weekend, Katy.

Child: I want to play to have fun.

Here is another Playful Child response, this time by Nancy. Again, notice the simplicity and straightforwardness of the Child's responses.

What do you want to do?

I want to go out to play
and have fun. I want to
be with friends and talk
and go to the beach and
to movies and for walks
I don't want to be
so serious. I want to go on
expeditions. I want to
make more friends.

Adult: What do you want to do?

Child: I want to go out to play and have fun. I want to be with friends and talk and go to the beach and to movies and for walks. I don't want to be so serious. I want to go on expeditions. I want to make more friends.

Be open to the genuine feeling of your Playful Child. Do not approach it with stereotypes. The Playful Child may not always want to be physically active or gregarious. Sometimes it may want to just hang out, be casual, and do nothing but indulge itself with good, clean fun. The following Playful Child conversation by Delores is a good example:

Adult: Well little one, what fun thing would you like to do tonight?

Child: I tired—I want to rest,
I want to play in water and wash
my hair and wear it down.
I want to call some friends
eat chocolate cake
and watch funny TV and laugh.

If you are having difficulty getting into a playful mood, take a look at your own Child of the Past. When you were a kid, you knew how to play in the simplest, most enjoyable ways.

PLAYFUL CHILD OF THE PAST

MATERIALS: Paper, felt pens, and crayons.

1.   With your non-dominant hand let your Inner Child write about a playful experience from your childhood.

2.   Let your Inner Child then draw a picture of the experience.

I liked to go to my Grampa's house. He let me sit on his lap while he listened to the hockey game on the radio. He didn't have any hair on his head. But he had some fuzzy stuff left. My Grama gave me little pieces of ribbon and string. I would tie them on his fuzzies. He looked cute all decorated up.

My Grama Laison used to go to church with us sometimes. I liked to sit on one side of her and my sister sat on the other side. Grama always wore her big brown fur coat. When we stood up to sing a song or say a prayer or something we would pretend we were giving her a pat on her back. What we were really doing was playing X's and O's on the fur coat. You had to be quick though because when she sat down she rubbed out our game. Grama didn't know about our trick. She just smiled at us and patted us back. My Mother would never have found out

if the nosey lady behind us hadn't
started to laugh. We weren't allowed
to do that any more on her coat so
we did it on her big chesterfield instead.
It was hard to keep people from
sitting on our game.

PROFESSIONAL WRESTLING

HIGH JUMPING

BOXING AT DOUG'S - I ALWAYS LOST

IN ART CLASS

PLAYING STRATEGO
AT STRO'S

PALS FOR LIFE

Humor, Laughter, and Play

It is generally recognized that humor and laughter have a healing effect on the body and mind. In his book *Anatomy of an Illness*, Norman Cousins describes how he healed himself from a so-called incurable disease by watching old comedy films. He literally laughed himself back to health.

We all know that laughter and humor *feel* good. We like to laugh, but we often forget to. Our Critical Parent takes over, and life becomes grim, humorless, dry, and dull. This is when burn-out sets in. We grow tired and lose our zest for life. At this point, it is easy to fall ill, and we may even be forced to drop out for a while.

After working with hundreds of individuals with chronic or life-threatening disease, I am convinced that illness is one way the Inner Child has of getting love and attention. The Inner Child feels so abandoned that its only recourse is to become sick so that the individual must stop whatever he or she is doing and go to bed. I have heard so many stories from overworked, overburdened adults whose bodies and psyches broke down in the face of too much responsibility that I have no doubt about the body/mind connection. If we will not listen to our Inner Child directly, the Child will speak indirectly, through illness. The choice is up to us.

LAUGHING

MATERIALS: Paper and felt pens.

1. Ask your Playful Child to tell you about all the ways that you can make room for more laughter and humor in your life. Let the Child write these ways down with your non-dominant hand.

2. With your dominant hand make a contract with your Playful Child regarding the things on its TO DO list. Write out exactly what you will do and when you will do the things it requested. Be sure to put these items on your calendar.

Here is an example of a Playful Child's list of ways to make room for laughter and fun. It was written with the non-dominant hand.

Spend time with people who like to laugh like Elliot, Fran, Jenny, Sherry, and Dean. Take the grandkids to the park, the playground & the beach.
Go to the comedy club.
Read Matt Groenig's books.
Go to funny movies.

One of the joys of parenting and grandparenting is the permission we get to hang out in playgrounds and other fun places. We use kids as an excuse for being messy, silly, childlike. It's the old "toy trains for the kids" syndrome, in which the father plays with the trains more than the kids do. But you do not need to have children or grandchildren in order to let your Inner Child out to play. All you need to do is give your Critical Parent a little vacation so you can relax and let your hair down.

Unfortunately, the only way that many adults can relax is through addictive or illegal behavior. Getting drunk or taking drugs become poor substitutes for experiencing one's Playful Child. The alcohol or drugs knock the Critical Parent aside long enough to let the Inner Child out. But, sooner or later, the Critical Parent returns with a vengeance, resuming control by putting the Inner Child down. It's a hopeless battle. Not until the Inner Child is healed and allowed to play in its own innocent and creative way can any real recovery take place. Technical sobriety is not recovery. Even the word— sobriety—has a seriousness about it that seems to exclude the Playful Child. True recovery, on the other hand, is about finding joyfulness within oneself, in that way that infants and children know joy from the core of their being.

PLAYGROUND

Find a friend or someone with whom your Playful Child feels free to express itself. Invite this individual to go to a playground, park, beach, or other environment where your Inner Children can come out to play. Go on the slide, climb the jungle gym, play on the swing or in the sandbox. If your Critical Parents are too judgmental about doing this when others are around, then find a time when you can have the place to yourselves.

DANCE PLAY

Find some recorded music that brings your Playful Child out. Let your Child express through full-body movement. Really let go. Imagine moving like a baby, a toddler, a young child. Let yourself crawl, walk, jump, skip, hop. Be spontaneous and let the music flow through your body and determine how you move.

YOUR PLAYFUL CHILD TODAY

Take your Inner Child to a toy store, an art supply store, a hardware store, or a hobby shop. Let your Inner Child pick out its favorite toy or playful activity. Give this to your Inner Child as a gift and find a special place to have fun playing. You might want to invite friends or loved ones to join you in doing this activity. It is especially fun to go to the store together and shop for your Inner Child.

Here are some suggested treats for your Playful Child:

Go to a playground.
Get some stuffed animals.
Get some of your favorite toys: e.g., dolls, toy trains, mechanical toys, building toys, dollhouses, squirt guns, yo-yos, kites, bubble-blowing rings and pipes, and hula hoops. Play with them.
Have a costume party.
Throw an Inner Child party (come as a kid, no grown-ups allowed) and ask guests to bring their favorite toys, games, and fun activities.
Give a party in a playground or park.
Buy some children's books and read them to yourself, or ask a friend to read one aloud to you. (*Winnie the Pooh* by A. A. Milne, *Where the Wild Things Are* by Maurice Sendak, and *The Velveteen Rabbit* by Margery Williams are popular choices.)
Play with paints, clay, Play-Doh, finger paint, chalks, and other art materials. Forget about a finished product; just enjoy exploring the materials.
Send funny notes to your Inner Child (written with your dominant hand).
Send funny notes to yourself from your Inner Child (written with your non-dominant hand).

Lucia, at age 39, unfettered and adventurous, on her skateboard.

James Ruebsamen, Santa Monica Evening Lookout

Drools of the game

Grown-ups make babies of themselves in college workshop

By Jon Markman
Herald Examiner staff writer

Lucia Capacchione, 43, asked Yves-Augustine "Choo-choo" Hopper, 2, to give the guest lecture at her Los Angeles City College workshop yesterday.

"Maa-mee," Choo-choo started, searching for words and sticking his blue paint-flecked right hand into his mouth. "Daa-dee," he added.

Choo-choo, who doesn't really talk yet, spent most of the rest of the afternoon gumming a chocolate chip cookie. But he was a considered a smash hit by his audience — a group of clay-sculpting, graham cracker-chewing, Oreo-splitting, fingerpainting adults who spent the day acting like children.

Capacchione, an art therapist, author and former nursery school teacher who came dressed from head to foot in purple, said she organized the workshop two years ago "for fun."

"I teach a class in creative diary writing and one day. I suggested we do a play day for grown-ups," she said, sitting cross-legged on the floor of the college's Women's Center, surrounded by down pillows, soft blankets, furry rattles and a baby bottle.

"It's a great therapy, a great release for repressed emotions and craziness. People who came in saying they can't paint and can't dance and can't sing and can't sculpt — do."

About 20 grown-ups — occupied during the week by such

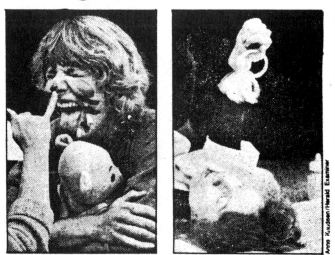

Christine Krainer gets her face painted while Tria Armstrong enjoys her pacifier and rattle at baby-for-a-day workshop yesterday.

adult matters as law practices, television script writing and magazine distribution — showed up at 9 a.m. to begin the workshop. Capacchione said the first thing many did was grab for her bags of food and toys.

She didn't stop them.

"We made two rules from the start," Robert "Bobby" Brenner, 44, said.

"First, no one was the teacher so no one had to ask permission to do anything. Second, no hitting."

Cuddling her head in a pillow while sucking her thumb languorously, Capacchione recounted the rest of the day.

"After we ate Oreos for breakfast, we painted, played with clay, ate a lot of peanut butter and jelly sandwiches on raisin bread, and ran into Thrifty's to buy squirt guns," she said, dous-

ing a friend with her Spiderman water pistol.

"Then we made faces at a psychology professor who came to take notes and tried to act grown-up with us, jumped rope and by that time, about 1 p.m., we were *soooo* tired — we took naps."

Harvey "Kiddo" Brenner, 51, a television script writer who has participated in previous Capacchione play days, reported the therapy helpful for his work.

"I find the child in me very free and the adult very restricted," he said, his head resting in a ready lap.

"A real releasing takes place here," he said. "The adult self comes away more creative for having played with the child self. And it's not just a shortlived thing. The one day of playing has a long-term residual effect on my work."

An article about "Play Day for Grown-Ups" appearing in the Los Angeles Herald Examiner *captured the spirit of the workshop.*

Play Day for Grown-Ups

"Play Day for Grown-Ups" is a workshop that has liberated many an Inner Child. As its name implies, it is a day for adults to play together like children. In putting on Play Days, I drew upon my background in early-childhood education. We started by transforming the environment (a student lounge at a local community college or a studio in a private home) into a nursery school. With finger paints, crayons, paper, clay, baby bottles, pacifiers, blankets, stuffed animals, bubble-blowing rings, squirt guns, and other childhood paraphernalia, we created a playful atmosphere. Snacks included kindergarten fare like graham crackers, peanut butter, cookies, and juice. We also had books such as the *The Velveteen Rabbit* or *Winnie-the-Pooh* for storytelling time before the inevitable afternoon nap.

These workshops often attracted extremely busy, responsible adults who somehow knew they needed to loosen up and let their Inner Child play. Among the participants it was typical to have doctors, lawyers, nurses, teachers, graduate students, writers, administrators, businesspeople, single parents, etc. In other words, these were very grown-up individuals who carried a full plate of duties that often felt like burdens.

The atmosphere was magical at these workshops. The groups were small, maybe a dozen or so, and people had permission to relax and truly let their Inner Child play. Often each person would choose a nickname to use at the workshop. Mine was Lulu. We had two rules: "No acting like a grown-up," and "No hitting or hurting anyone or the environment."

Participants were very creative. One woman brought a suitcase full of make-up, and face-painting became a popular activity. At another Play Day we celebrated Maureen's birthday. The birthday girl arrived at ten A.M. in costume (a pink ballerina's tutu), carrying her own birthday cake. As soon as she placed it on the table, we sang "Happy Birthday" and then attacked the cake with our bare hands, just as two-year-olds would. We literally laughed until we cried.

The feedback from these workshops was magnificent. At the end of the day, participants described their experiences with terms like: liberated, unburdened, light, unfettered, creative, adventurous, silly, accepted, being my real self, really having fun, childlike, just playing around, dropping the adult role, grateful to feel my Inner Child, feeling safe to be vulnerable, and determined to keep my Inner Child alive.

The Playful Child and the Retirement Years

For many people, retirement is a difficult time. Without the structure of a job and the identity of a familiar career role, some individuals literally fall apart. Years and years of working a 9-to-5 job or being in business for oneself do not train a person for the open, unstructured days of retirement. Time that could be filled with fun, new adventures, and harvesting the rewards of one's hard work often seems a gaping hole, a huge question mark.

Actually, retirement can open up all kinds of delightful possibilities if the Playful Child is allowed to emerge and to provide vitality and new zest for life. A case in point is Geri Towle. Geri had spent many years working as a social worker, as a commercial grower of orchids, and as a wife and mother of two sons. When their children were grown, Geri and her husband, Dick, sold their orchid business and their home and waited for what to do next.

Geri began working with my book *The Power of Your Other Hand* and discovered her Inner Child. She soon bought a charming picture of a little girl holding a kitten and a woman standing in front of a quaint little English cottage. There were kittens frolicking in the garden at the child's feet. This scene warmed the heart of Geri's Inner Child. Later, Geri and I had a private session. After she shared more about the discovery she had made through written dialogues, I asked Geri if I could talk to her Inner Child. She immediately moved to a corner of the porch swing where she was sitting and became "little Geri." Her face relaxed into an expression of openness and innocence as she told me of the things she liked to do. There was a sparkle in Geri's eyes when she told me of her deep love of horses and the joy she had experienced while horseback-riding as a child. She told how as a teenager she had become an avid rider and appeared in horse shows. Then a dark cloud of sadness passed over her face as she recounted that one day, without warning, her horses were sold. Geri's heart was broken. Her Playful Child went underground. She put away the things of a child and went on to become a responsible adult, but something very precious was lost in the process.

In our interview "little Geri" was finally able to express her deeply held secret wish: to own a horse again and rediscover the joy of riding. Geri's face lit up as "little Geri" talked about her love of horses, what good friends they had been, and what great fun and freedom she had experienced on horseback.

A few days later Geri called to share her good news. She and Dick had bought a horse from a leading breeder and trainer of Arabian horses. The next time I visited them, they took me out to see their new "prize." What a beautiful animal! And what a magnificent way for Geri to honor her Inner

One year after beginning Inner Child Work, Geri beams with happiness.

Once again a confident horsewoman, Geri can be seen astride her prize-winning Arabian, Comment.

Child. As she introduced me to the horse, Geri was giggling and bubbling over with joy, just like a little kid. "Little Geri" was in her element and big Geri looked at least ten years younger than the last time I had seen her. There is no doubt about it: letting your Playful Child out is a great way to stay young.

A few months later Geri bought Dick a set of building blocks. Of course, the blocks were really for Dick's Inner Child, who enjoyed them immensely. A few weeks later, Geri asked her husband and her brother to remember what

A year after discovering her Inner Child, Geri fulfilled her childhood dream and showed her own horse. She won first prize in her category.

Geri proudly displays her first-prize ribbon.

it had been like when as small children they had gone to the toy store and had not been able to get what they really wanted. She asked them to recall the feeling of disappointment and longing. Then she exclaimed, "Today we are going to the toy store and you can let your Inner Kid get the toy you always wanted." She then took them both to the toy store, where Dick picked a toy tractor with a scoop on it, her brother got a dump truck, and Geri got herself a set of jacks and pick-up-sticks, and a truck pulling a horse trailer with two horses in it. They all went home and played on the living room floor for hours, just like kids.

AWARENESS

With your dominant hand, write out your observations about your Playful Child. What role does it play in your life? Review the exercises you did. What did you discover? Is the Playful Child active in your life? If so, where? If not, how can it be included?

This Creative Child's name is Mary Sue—Lou Lou.
She throws her flowers and steps lively.

T E N
Celebrating Your Creative Child

Genius is childhood recaptured.

—CHARLES BAUDELAIRE

Every child is an artist. The problem is how to remain an artist once he grows up.

—PABLO PICASSO

The truly great artist has the eyes of a child, and the vision of a sage.

—PABLO CASALS

Creativity is our birthright. We are born with it. Children are naturally creative, imaginative, and resourceful. They have to be in order to survive. I say this from years of experience observing, teaching, and photographing hundreds of pre-school children of all socioeconomic backgrounds. But somewhere down the line something goes wrong. In elementary school the creative spark begins to fade, and by adulthood it is almost extinguished.

When I ask adults to draw in my workshops, the vast majority of them panic. They say they can't draw and have no creative talent. Remedial work is required to help them relax. They need to give their Critical Parent a break and make it safe for the Creative Child to come out. For the Creative Child can draw. It can dance. It can sing. It can invent. It can write. It can discover. The Critical Parent Within, however, obsessed with looking good and being in control, is too threatened to allow experimentation, because that could lead to ''mistakes.'' But it is precisely through experimentation that the Creative Child lives and breathes. The Creative Child must be allowed to be messy, to explore new possibilities and make ''mistakes.'' Actually, for the Creative Child there are no mistakes, there are only discoveries.

In this chapter we revisit that magical world of the Creative Child that we left behind so long ago. It is here that our dreams are born. For our *true* wishes come from the heart of the Creative Child. The spirit of the Creative Child knows no bounds. It can fly to the stars, it can plumb the depths of the human soul. It is fueled by an inexhaustible supply of enthusiasm and imagination. When we are suffering with a creative block of any kind, it is the Creative Child who is being held captive.

Sometimes, when we dialogue with the Inner Child, it is clearly the creative aspect speaking. In this conversation, Cara's Creative Child came out and told what it wanted in very specific terms. Then the Child illustrated its words by creating a symbolic self-portrait, a free and fully open flower.

Adult: How do you want to come out or express more in my life?

Child: I want you to keep writing because then I get to come out. I love to play with you & draw pictures. I will unfold in your life like a flower if you water me with love and attention. I love you. I want to channel my love thru you in music and poetry & writing. I am your guiding light and your guardian angel. This is me.

you in music & poetry & writing. I am your guiding light & your guardian angel. This is me.

Nancy is an inspiring example of a woman whose Creative Child finally expressed itself after lying dormant for many years. As a young girl, Nancy had an unexplainable desire to have an art portfolio. She had no logical reason, for she was not studying art and had nothing to put in such a portfolio. As an English major in college, Nancy began frequenting museums with her best friends, who were majoring in Art History. A new world of color and form opened up to her and she began taking Art History classes herself. However, Nancy's appreciation of art remained at the level of a spectator. Her Critical Parent had very opinionated ideas about who should and should not attempt to do artwork. There was no room for practice and mistakes. You were born with genius and talent or you were not. This left no room for Nancy's Creative Child to take its first steps in exploring the creative process.

Years passed as Nancy immersed herself in the world of communications and media. In her mid-thirties Nancy showed up one day in my weekly women's group. She quickly took to journal writing and drawing and soon discovered a very artistic Creative Child in her non-dominant hand.

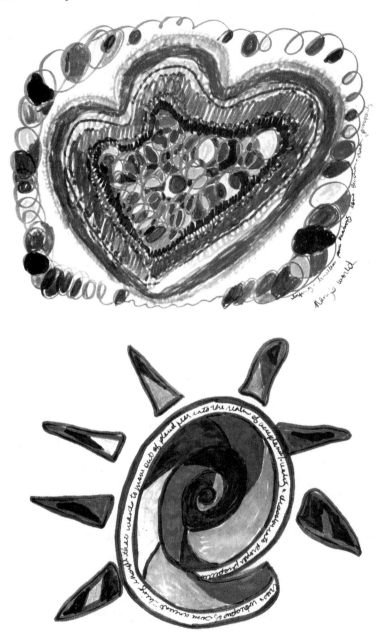

A chain reaction of life changes followed after the discovery of Nancy's Creative Child. She left a high-pressure job on a top-ranked television series and eventually went into business for herself as a media, art, and publishing consultant. And perhaps most important, she fulfilled a lifetime dream: to fill a portfolio with her own artwork. Nancy's passion became the weekly art classes she attended. Her Creative Child was allowed free reign in many forms and media. With her right hand she now experiences as much joy and satisfaction in drawing and painting as she did with her left hand in the journal. With delight she is now creating human and animal forms, as well as still lifes, something that seemed impossible before. Nancy found that the secret to entering the world of the Creative Child is in "leaving the Critical Parent at the door." In a letter, she described her art experiences as follows:

> The key to creative expression for me is observing closely what I am seeing, and at the same time immersing myself in its feeling. Continuing to observe and feel I loose myself and become one with what I am drawing or painting. This process also includes taking chances and risks, making mistakes and trusting my intuition over logical or intellectual choices. I know I have succeeded creatively when I have stayed true to the step-by-step process, rather than being concerned with having a beautiful outcome that I had constructed in my mind.

Creativity In Childhood

Often when people tell me they are untalented or uncreative, I ask them to recall some of the imaginative things they loved to do as kids. What did they dream of doing or becoming? Where did they go on their flights of fantasy into the realm of unlimited possibilities? When they share their reminiscences, incredible stories pour out. Kevin described building clubhouses with his buddies in the backyard, elaborate structures made of shipping cartons, orange crates, barrels, and other "refuse." Paul and his best friend wrote a play on their own one summer and performed it at an elementary school the following semester. Jacqueline, whose family was very poor, made her own dolls out of fabric scraps from her mother's sewing box. Two sisters, Liz and Laura, spent hours on cold winter days constructing an entire world of stuffed animals, dolls, and toys in their bedroom. They made up stories with characters and complex plots that went on for weeks, like a TV series. Gary spent hours roaming around the woods, lakes, and streams, and even more hours drawing pictures of what he loved in nature.

After telling such stories, people frequently express sadness. They feel cheated. This magical, whimsical part of themselves got lost somewhere. It was there once upon a time. "What happened to it?" they ask. "Is this the price we have to pay for growing up?" Have you ever wondered what it would be like if you could have continued being as creative as you were in childhood? What would life be like if you cultivated your Creative Child? How would it feel to have visions and (instead of dismissing them as impractical) make them a reality? IT FEELS GREAT. I know, because I have been doing just that all my life. I did it first as an artist, then as an educational curriculum developer, later as a product designer and filmmaker, and now as a facilitator, therapist, and author.

I was blessed to have been born into a family and Italian subculture that valued the arts. In those pre-television days, we went to operas, plays, concerts, musical comedies, and ballets. From my earliest years, I was taken to movies and art museums. Long before the term Inner Child was invented, I knew that the child spirit was the secret to creativity. As a kid, I saw the Inner Child in action. I did not have a name for it, but I knew it when I saw it. My father, a film editor at MGM studios during the forties took me to sound stages and sneak previews of the musicals he worked on: *Meet Me in St. Louis, Till the Clouds Roll By, Ziegfeld Follies,* and *Harvey Girls.* Yes, there was mastery and profound artistic discipline—the hard work of the adult self. But the spark, the entertainment value, came from the Creative Child in all those singers, dancers, directors, set designers, etc. Many of the performers were still children when they became stars, like Judy Garland, Mickey Rooney, and Elizabeth Taylor.

At home I was surrounded by master craftswomen. My mother (who had worked as a seamstress for Beverly Hills couturiers and for the MGM wardrobe department) was making clothes for private clients, for me, and for my dolls. My mother's mother (trained as a tailor in Italy) had been widowed at an early age and made her living creating clothes for Italian weddings. With as many as twelve women and girls in the bridal party, not to mention relatives of the bride and groom, such a project might involve twenty or more elaborately designed gowns. And they were all made next to the simmering pots of spaghetti sauce, in the kitchen of my grandmother's Victorian home.

Movies or weddings, MGM sound stages or grandma's kitchen, it was all show business. And even then, I knew it was the grown-ups playing dress-up, the way we kids did in the summer months. That was the time when my pals and I got together and put on plays in our garage, without any interference from parents or teachers. We wrote scripts, made costumes, painted backdrops, printed programs and tickets, advertised to the neighbors, and put on gala performances for the huge sum of one dime. It was our world—all kids, no adults. We got to make it up as we went along. We were in youthful bliss. There was no need to read books or take workshops in creativity. We were doing what came naturally.

At an early age I knew my life would be devoted to the arts. I felt that if I could not express myself through the arts, I would rather be dead. When I asked for piano lessons at age eight, I got them. Later, when I requested art lessons, my mother enrolled me in Saturday painting classes. Music and art saved my sanity during those difficult teenage years in Catholic girls' high schools. I am eternally grateful to my parents for nurturing the Creative Child in me. I could not have asked for more support. By college, I was ready to strike out on my own unique path.

In looking back, it is clear that it was my search for the spirit of the Creative Child that influenced my choice of mentors when I attended college as an art major. I'd like to share what I learned about creativity straight from the horse's mouth—some giants in the field of art, design, and architecture. My motto has been, "If you're going to learn something, find the very best teacher there is on the subject." I learned about creativity not from scientific observers, textbooks, or research studies, but from being around people whose Creative Child was very much alive.

Genius and the Creative Child

Sister Mary Corita (later known as Corita Kent) was a nun, an artist, and an instructor at Immaculate Heart College in Hollywood during the fifties and sixties. She embodied the child spirit. A tiny woman, she resembled a leprechaun in nun's garb. She had the magical spark of the Creative Child.

As an artist Corita was a trailblazer, and as a teacher she was a great inspiration, but it was her Inner Child that attracted me to study with her.

Corita was a paradox. Both as an artist and a teacher she had a thoroughly unconventional style, yet she lived within the confines of a Catholic convent. Within those boundaries, however, her life and her work were about "play." She played on paper with bright colors, bold strokes, and thought-provoking works from e. e. cummings, Walt Whitman, and the Bible. She played with environments—exhibits of art mounted on corrugated shipping cartons and mosaics on old plumbing in the convent basement. She also played with her Catholicism, orchestrating high-spirited religious celebrations. Wearing flowered wreaths over her veil, she joined us in carrying pop art banners in processions amidst the sound of the Beatles singing "She loves you—yah yah yah—she loves you—yah yah yah."

Corita left the convent in the late sixties but her work continued. She became internationally known as Corita Kent, with work in galleries, museums, and international-fair pavilions throughout the world. She created calendars, posters, murals, designs for urban water tanks. However, she is best known for her smallest work: a famous U.S. postal stamp that appeared in 1986, the year she died. The word "LOVE" appears in purple, childlike print. Floating above is a rainbow made of multicolored brush strokes. That image summed up Corita's spirit and style—simple, to the point, colorful and loving from a child's heart. It is no accident that she was given the name Corita when she became a nun: it is Latin for "little heart."

My next mentor was another magical child masquerading as an adult: Charles Eames, pioneer of modern furniture and exhibit design. My first glimpse of Eames's special world was in a film documenting his now-famous home—a high-tech glass and steel structure nestled in a meadow overlooking the Pacific Ocean.

This seemingly stark geometric building formed the backdrop for the Eames collection of personal treasures. Alongside Charles's ultra-modern metal, fiberglass, and molded plywood chairs there were artfully arranged displays of seashells, toys, and folk art from around the world. From exquisite close-ups of flowers to abstract rain patterns on windows, this film (produced and photographed by Charles and his wife, Ray) looks at life through the delighted eyes of a child. Some of the objects were the kinds of things children collect, yet they were so beautifully arranged, I did not think real children could be living in this house. I remember asking Sister Corita, in whose class the film was shown, if there were any kids living there. She twinkled and answered, "Only the Eameses (meaning Charles and Ray.)"

At the end of class, I marched up to Corita and announced, "I'm going to work for Eames someday. What do I have to do?" Pausing to assess whether I really meant it, Corita advised, "Stay here. Work hard, get your degree, and then we'll talk about it." Then, almost as an aside, she said, "The Eameses are friends of ours." Following her guidance, I fulfilled my dream and went to work at the Eames office.

Ironically, my first assignment was baby-sitting Charles's three visiting grandchildren (ages two, four, and five) at the house that I had seen in the film. Then I went to work at the Eames's Venice studio which has been documented in John and Marilyn Newharts' book, *Eames Design,* and in the Demetrios film *901.* The Eames office was housed in an old automotive garage in the heart of a ghetto. Nondescript on the outside, the inside danced with child spirit. Its interior barnlike space had been divided into separate work areas with moveable walls. There was furniture being developed in one area, models for exhibit designs in another corner, and a photo darkroom off to the side. Graphic design projects and film production filled up all the "empty" spaces. It was a wonderland, a melange of projects in process, photos, artwork, toys, and other amusements. Mostly, it was a huge, glittering playpen for big kids who were serious about play and playful about everything they did. My three years at the Eames office taught me that true genius comes from the Playful and Creative Child Within combined with the devotion and discipline of a master craftsman.

My next mentors were a classroom of inner-city fourth graders in central Los Angeles. The scene was an old parochial school and the cast was made up of forty-eight kids, mostly Latino and black. On a whim, I left the Eames office and accepted a teaching job, even though I had no training or experience. I think the principal was desperate, and I know I was too young and ignorant to know what I had gotten myself into. I finally recovered from the shock of facing a class of forty-eight kids, and it turned out to be one of the most demanding but rewarding few months of my life. After a difficult start, as I struggled with whether to be a disciplinarian (like the nuns who taught me in grammar school) or an artist (like Corita), the artist won out. I began teaching everything through art: math, geography, English, religion. The kids loved it. So I kept doing it. By the end of the semester, the students had all improved their grades and the class was honored in a Los Angeles City Schools art festival: all four prizes in their category.

Two of my later teachers in creativity were my own daughters, Celia and Aleta, who were born shortly after my stint as a schoolteacher. Here and there, other adults have come along who have led creative lives and who have shown me, once again, that the source of genius in us all is the Creative Child Within. Some of them are not well known; others are, like Bucky Fuller (philosopher and inventor of the geodesic dome). Once Bucky told me he discovered many of his design concepts while in kindergarten, building structures with peas and toothpicks. Another adult with an active Creative Child was a ninety-year-old woman who came to Play Day for Grown-Ups in costume. She sang songs with original lyrics and put everyone else to shame when it came to really knowing how to have a good time. If there had been a Young at Heart prize, she would have won it.

I share these stories with you because I want to demystify creativity. It is not the province of a privileged few. It is something we all have. These stories have provided behind-the-scenes glimpses of some highly creative adults who have received recognition as leaders in their fields. Yes, they worked hard. Yes, they had perseverance. These are necessary ingredients for great accomplishments. But without the Creative Child Within, there would have been no charisma, no playfulness, no inspiration, no vision—only technical proficiency. I believe it is the Creative Child in us who takes us to the stars and to the depths of our True Self.

If you are burdened with a belief system that says, "I'm not creative. I have no talent," it may help for you to revisit that natural creativity you had as a kid. The next exercise will help you to find that Creative Child you were in your early years—the part of you who could invent, solve problems, and make your visions a reality.

CREATIVE CHILD OF THE PAST

MATERIALS: Paper, crayons, and felt pens.

1. Think of a time in childhood when you invented something or did something creative, when you used your imagination to create imaginary worlds, to solve problems, or to express your deepest feelings.

2. With your non-dominant hand draw a picture of yourself as a child doing something creative.

3. Continuing to use your non-dominant hand, let your Creative Child write about the experience.

4. Ask your Creative Child of the Past to write a poem about itself with your non-dominant hand.

I had my own car when I was only 4 years old. I put a gas tank on my wagon. I punched a little hole in a tin can and tied it to the back of the wagon. Then I would fill up the can with water. I could go a long way up the street before I ran out of gas. Everywhere I went I left a little trail of water. We had to do this outside because my Mother wouldn't let me bring my car in the house.

Your Creative Child of the Past is still alive, believe it or not. It can be revived and brought into your everyday life—now! It can express in the way you dress, cook, decorate your home, or design your garden. It can come out in your hobbies, avocations, or personal passions, such as travel, the arts, sports, collecting, etc. It can enliven and expand the horizons of your work, bringing freshness and innovation. It provides the uniqueness and originality that make for distinctiveness and leadership in any field. And the Creative Child brings the spark that makes work fun and life worth living.

CREATIVE CHILD

MATERIALS: Paper, crayons, pastels, and felt pens.

1. With your non-dominant hand draw a picture of your Creative Child.

2. Write a dialogue with your Creative Child. The Child writes with your non-dominant hand; you write with your dominant hand. Ask your Creative Child how it feels in your life right now. Is it active? Or is it in the closet? What does it like to do, how does it like to feel? What can you do to bring it into your life?

Mary Jo wrote the following dialogue with her Creative Child in a weekend workshop. In the midst of a career transition, Mary Jo was going to school at the time and was feeling greatly overextended due to the pressures of the academic environment. She desperately needed to balance her life with some quality fun time.

Adult: What do you want to do creatively?

Creative Child: I want to be able to draw or paint. I don't get to do anything like art, dance or music now. It would be nice to sit outside in the woods or at the beach and draw people, boats and everything.

The following is a drawing and dialogue by Sue Maxwell, the artist whose drawings of children appeared earlier. Obviously her Creative "magical" Child is very healthy and alive.

Adult: Where do you live?

Magical Child: Yonder—in sky's night—where birds take flight—where flight—where the songs of the moon—creamy white sing you a lullaby good night—where the owl hoots his fright song to the little scavengers of the night. Where star strings reach down with silken filaments to tangle with your hair—that's where, I live, that's where.

Adult: Do you travel back and forward in time? Where do you go?

Magical Child: I go too slow, where no man knows, to a time where I climb into a time when man was not yet on this earth. Too slow it goes, too slow. I go fast to the past when life was a matter of molecules and silver spatter—no matter, I paint with my nose all the colors of rainbows—I see—my knees climb the trees—watch the bees—if you please. I chatter and patter at the moon—so soon—its the song of the loon.

WISHES AND DREAMS

MATERIALS: Paper, crayons, pastels, and felt pens.

1. Ask your Creative Child to draw a picture of something it would like to do, express, or experience. Do the drawing with the non-dominant hand.

2. With your non-dominant hand do a second drawing. This time show your Creative Child *after* it has achieved its wish. Perhaps it has accomplished a creative task, developed a new skill, or broken through its fear and succeeded in overcoming an obstacle.

The next two drawings were done in a workshop. This woman's Creative Child wanted to express herself through art. Notice the exuberance of the Child in her second picture. When dreams come true new zest for life is released.

Delores attended a workshop in which we explored the Creative Child's heart's desire. When you read her dialogue it will be obvious that the fulfillment of her Creative Child's wishes and dreams is a powerful path to healing.

Adult: Little one if you were to create something what would it be?

Child: Well I like to write and draw.

Adult: If you could do something right now, what would it be?

Child: That's easy! I want to make my very own baby book. I want to put pictures of me—pictures I draw and write stories like Raggedy Ann and Andy and teddy bear stories and all kinds.

When Delores read this dialogue to the group she explained that the children in her family had never had baby books. This was something she had

always wanted. So part of her re-parenting process involved her Inner Parent making a baby book for her Inner Child.

Don's Creative Child was very musical and also quite gregarious. When asked what it wanted to do right now it said, "Play music and share it with a special person." His Creative Child also said it wanted to show love. Here are the two pictures that he did showing his Creative Child before and after receiving his heart's desire.

The Creative Child and Your Career

In my own career I have been forced to deal with creative blocks time and time again. Over the years, in order to conceive and produce a wide range of work, such as posters, greeting cards, films, toys, and books, I've had to hurdle many barriers. Some of these barriers were external. For instance, for many years I could not find publishers for my books. I had to be patient and continue working, in spite of rejection and delays. But most of the obstacles were internal. My Critical Parent ridiculed me mercilessly for even attempting to be an author. It heckled and jeered with phrases like, "You're no author. You can't write. No publisher will ever accept this." The rejection letters from editors seemed to confirm the Critical Parent's opinion. Without this precious tool, the technique of dialoguing with my Creative Child, I seriously doubt if I could have continued to write books all those years. In fact, it was my Creative Child who insisted that we get our books out there by self-publishing. She wanted to keep writing and creating.

As an art therapist and corporate consultant, my specialty has been the creative process. I am constantly being asked, "How can I unblock? How do I get out of the way of my creative abilities?" My answer: by creating safety and respect for the Creative Child Within. And that is what we have been doing in this book. All the activities, examples, and explanations have been leading us to our Creative Child. For by listening to the feelings of the Inner Child, by nurturing and protecting that Child, and by dealing effectively with the Critical Parent, we make it safe for the Creative Child to come out of hiding and to blossom.

TAKING YOUR CREATIVE CHILD TO WORK

MATERIALS: Paper and felt pens.

1. Ask your Creative Child how it currently expresses itself in your work. What are the situations where it feels welcome or even a necessary part of your work activities? Ask the questions with your dominant hand and let your Creative Child answer with your non-dominant hand.

2. Continue the dialogue with your Creative Child. Ask what areas of your work it feels left out of. What situations make it feel uncomfortable, unwelcome, overlooked, or totally abandoned?

3. Now ask your Creative Child how it would *like* to express itself more in your work life? How would it change your work life if it could have its say? Change jobs? Change careers? New role or position? Different work conditions? Different environment?

4. With your non-dominant hand, let your Creative Child draw a picture of itself in a work situation, being as creative, expressive, inventive, and imaginative as it can be.

Chris, a successful author, did a short but powerful conversation with his Inner Child. He received wonderful guidance on how to restore his creative juices.

Adult: What do you need?

Child: I need a lot of love and understanding right now. Things are changing so quickly. Growth is so rapid. Sometimes it delights me. Other times it scares me. I need more fun time and play time. Time just to be with Chris. Give me that time and I'll give you all you want and need.

Alison attended a workshop where she dialogued with her creativity—the Magical Child. She received clear guidelines about work, health, play, and home.

Adult: Who are you?

Child: I am the magical child.

Adult: How can I use your energy in my career?

Child: I am your career. You're a poet & painter, not a student. Get your priorities right. No more office work. & I don't want to teach literature either. I heard that "artists starve" remark. Tell that to Lucia and Louise Hay.

Adult: How can I let you come out in my relationships?

Child: Stand up for me with family. Avoid critical people. Find people who like me. Bring me out more with your friends. Find more people like Marianne.

Adult: How can you help keep me healthy?

Child: Let me laugh. Don't take health and self improvement so seriously. It's a process, not a race. Enjoy it.

Adult: How do you want to spend our leisure time?

Child: What leisure time? You always want to read Trungpa whenever we get a spare minute. Life shouldn't all be "good for you." I know you're a snob, but how bout a movie or some tv? How bout an evening w/friends who aren't trying so hard to be enlightened. I want more Dr. Seuss books!

Adult: What shall I do to our environment?

Child: I like the crystals—they're fun & pretty. Want more colors. Want soft fuzzy things. Want a lava lamp. Shut up—I don't care how much it costs! Want pillows. Want Cat in the Hat. Want Goofy and Pluto. Want black and white. ant pillows shaped like starfishes. Want a puppy. Want a seal in the bathtub, or a penguin. Want big huge glow in the dark dinosaurs. Want a swing set. Want a clown with balloons. Want big red striped clothes.

Joan did a before-and-after drawing related to her new career direction. In the dialogue that followed, her Creative Child stated very clearly what kind of work it wants to do.

Adult: Hi Creative Child!

Child: Hi, Joanie! Its about time! Your 54 and you've just acknowledged me.

Adult: Yeah, I know! But finally I've come to ask, "What is your heart's desire?"

Child: You already know. I want you to be a college professor and write bilingual children's stories and complete your idea stories. . . .

Adult: I'll work on it starting today! What will you look like when its accomplished.

The next series of activities is messy. Giving yourself permission to be messy is a big step toward accepting your Creative Child and letting it express in its own way. For many adults this is not easy to do. The more responsible and the more "grown-up" you are, the more difficult it may be for you to do this exercise. Your Critical Parent may start yelling about how stupid and childish this is, how foolish you would look to the people who know (and respect) you. Your Critical Parent might start telling you what a waste of time and money this is and that you'll probably ruin your clothes with all this paint, etc., ad nauseam. If this happens, simply be aware of that voice and go on with what you're doing. If the Critical Parent gets too loud, you may want to stop and have a written dialogue with it. Let the Critical Parent say what it has to say with your dominant hand. Then give equal time to your Playful Child (writing with your non-dominant hand) and let it speak up for what it wants. Then it's up to you to make the final decision about how to proceed.

EXPRESSING YOUR CREATIVE CHILD

MATERIALS: Large-newsprint paper (18″ x 24″), felt pens, magazines with photos, scissors, glue, crayons, pastels, and colored paper.

1. In the center of your paper draw a picture of your Creative Child or glue in a photo of yourself from childhood if it expresses your creativity.

2. With photos from the magazines and through drawing, create a picture showing how your Creative Child would like to express itself in all areas of your life: your physical health, leisure, hobbies, social life, home environment, work, the arts, etc.

3. On a separate sheet of paper, let your Creative Child write a poem about itself and what it wants from you at this time.

FINGER PAINTS

MATERIALS: Finger paints, paper, appropriate clean-up supplies, and work area, e.g., garage, kitchen, outdoors. Optional: newsprint paper.

1. Have fun smooshing around with finger paints. Get messy, enjoy the sensory experience—the thick texture of the paint on your finger and on the paper. Explore the colors and the movement of your hands across the page.

2. With your non-dominant hand let your Playful Child draw a picture of itself with the finger paints. You can make a print to save by blotting a piece of newsprint paper onto the painting.

NOTE: Finger paints and special finger-paint paper are available in art supply stores and some hobby shops.

CLAY PLAY

MATERIALS: Clay, work surface (masonite or wooden board), paper towels and other clean-up supplies, and appropriate work area, e.g., garage, kitchen, outdoors. Use only wet ceramic clay for this exercise.

1. With your eyes closed, play with the clay. See how many things you can do with it: knead it, roll it into balls and snakes, flatten it out into pancakes, poke your fingers into it, etc. . . . Do not try to make art or any recognizable subject matter. The reason for keeping your eyes closed is so that you will not judge or evaluate your work based on appearances. This activity is process-oriented, not product-oriented. The process is the sensory experience, the feel of the clay, and what you can do with it physically, not aesthetically. Aesthetics come later.

2. Continue playing with the clay with your eyes closed, but this time make a shape or form that feels good to your hands and fingers and that feels good emotionally. Again, your intention here is to focus on sensory experience, so do not picture a subject in your mind. This is not about representing anything in the outer world or creating a symbol of any kind.

3. When you feel finished open your eyes and look at what you have done. Without intending it, you may have formed something that reminds you of an experience of the outer world. One woman ended up with an image that looked like an infant, although she had never intended that while playing with the clay; she only discovered that image when she opened her eyes. A man created a perfect seashell form without realizing it until he looked at his work. The point is to let your hands play with the clay without trying to perform or produce something that "looks good" to the Inner Critic.

4. Let your Creative Child make a sculpture in clay of anything it wants to express to you. Let it "speak" to you through the clay.

5. Let your sculpture dry out in the sun (or bake it in a hot oven) so that it hardens, and display it where you can see it.

MIXED MEDIA

MATERIALS: Paper, crayons, pastels, colored paper, scissors, glue, and magazines with photographs.

Let your Creative Child make a picture using one or all of the media listed above. Or add other materials, if you wish. Allow the Child to make any kind of picture it wants.

FOUND-OBJECT SCULPTURES

MATERIALS: Found objects ("stuff" that is lying around the house and you don't need, e.g., toilet paper or paper-towel rolls, TV dinner tray, plastic muffin wrapping, Styrofoam packing ["pop corn"], corrugated cardboard, paper clips, wire, colored paper, thread spools, or things from nature such as seashells, leaves, stones, twigs, feathers, etc.).

1. Let your Creative Child make a piece of sculpture with the found objects. Let the Child express anything it wants to in this sculpture.

2. Display your sculpture where you can see it. You may even want to add to it as time goes on.

CREATIVE CHILD PARTY

Have a party celebrating everyone's Creative Child. Pick a theme. Ask people to wear clothes or costumes according to your theme. Here are some suggestions:

1. An Inner Child party. Come as a child of any age—infant to age eight.

2. A What Do You Want to Be When You Grow Up party. Come as the

person your Inner Child would like to be—an astronaut, ballet dancer, etc.

Make it a potluck party and ask people to be creative with their culinary contributions. Have someone take photos of each person as a souvenir of the party.

AWARENESS

With your dominant hand, write down what you noticed about your Creative Child. Is it alive and well? Or is it in the closet? If your Creative Child is active, where does it express in your life? Where would your Creative Child like to come out more?

"trailing clouds of glory
do we come from God...."
(Wm. Wordsworth)

Sue

ELEVEN

Discovering Your Spiritual Child

Living deep within each of us is a Spiritual Child. This is the Holy Infant, the beloved baby, the innocent child who lives in love. This part of us knows nothing of an ego that is split off from God, from nature, from others, or from itself. It knows a far greater reality than the personality. It helps us surrender to our Higher Power, the God Within—for it sees with its heart. With an inner knowing, the Spiritual Child speaks in the silence of our soul. It talks to us in simple words, with clarity and eternal wisdom. As we heal the Inner Child, we find the Spiritual Child waiting there within our very own heart.

In order to truly appreciate this Spiritual Child's essence, it is helpful to hear it speak directly. In one of my Inner Child workshops at a retreat center, a woman dialogued with her Spiritual Child, who wrote:

I want you to meet me in the silence each morning. I have answers you need and you can best make that contact when you're quiet. Come to me when you have challenges. . . . I am the Christ child—I am the way to heal conflict. I am the answer. Come to me when you are weary and I will give you rest.

No matter how painful our childhood may have been, the Spiritual Child was residing within, whether we knew it or not. And it is still there waiting to give us a gift: the innocence and enthusiasm we so sorely need. This is the Child of God in us radiating with light and joy. The Spiritual Child knows the truth: that it is being sustained by an unlimited source of divine love. You can get a glimpse of the Spiritual Child in the face of any infant who is expressing what Joseph Campbell calls "the rapture of being alive." Sadly, the Spiritual Child becomes obscured by our preoccupation with the surface of life. When we focus on how we appear to others, how we can manipulate and control the world around us, we lose sight of our Spiritual Child. And we lose touch with our divine Self: our Higher Power or God Within.

The Spiritual Child appears naturally in many ways. It can be found in meditation, in prayer, and in contemplation. We may sense its presence while enjoying a starry night or a breathtaking view from a mountaintop. The Spiritual Child is our sense of wonder at the vastness of the sky and the depth of the ocean. It is the feeling of awe at the exquisite perfection of an unfolding rose. The Spiritual Child is that still small voice calling us home to our Inner Self.

The Spiritual Child—the whole and healed infant or youngster—sometimes comes to us in the dream state. This is a time when the rational mind steps aside and allows a deeper wisdom to speak. For centuries, humanity has known that guidance comes in dreams. In the Bible, we read of dreams that brought prophecies and teachings. In modern therapeutic treatment, dreams are used for accessing hidden messages from within the psyche. We often ignore these precious messages, because dreams appear to be irrational and impractical. But if we are willing to take the time, dreams can be an important place to contact the Spiritual Child.

The Inner Child in Dreams

Children appear in our dreams at night in a variety of ages, forms, and moods. A child in dreams signifies different things at different times. Sometimes we are giving birth or witnessing an infant being born. This usually indicates that some new quality or dormant part of our personality is emerging.

As Adele was starting a new career (which later brought her much happiness and success), she had several dreams of giving birth to a boy. She was actually the mother of three girls. In reflecting upon these dreams Adele saw that the infant boy symbolized a newly emerging masculine part of her psyche (Jung called this a woman's animus). Prior to this period, Adele's work life had been a stress-filled struggle that led to burn-out. Her succession of boring jobs had felt like drudgery. Her inner masculine image had appeared in dreams as a tired, old, or feeble man. Now the masculine image was revealing itself as an exuberant baby starting life anew. Adele felt that finding the right career had given her "a new lease on life," ushered in by the newborn infant in her dreams. Sometimes, a child dream can show us how to heal our Inner Child. In fact, we can actually ask our Inner Self to guide us in the re-parenting process through our dreams. Lori, a young woman in her mid-thirties, was suffering with several physical ailments, including gynecological problems, severe anemia, and chronic fatigue. She had a pattern of co-dependence in which she rescued others: family members, friends, and employers. Lori herself came last, and her Inner Child was screaming out in the form of illness.

In a private session I told Lori my definition of co-dependence: "When your Inner Parent (both Nurturing and Protective) takes care of everyone else's Inner Child and abandons your own Child Within." Lori smiled with a look of recognition and told me about a series of dreams she had just had. She had learned the technique of requesting guidance from her Inner Self by asking for a dream that would show her the path to healing.

Dream # 1: The Child Locked in the Car

My mother and I were walking down a hallway after taking an elevator when I realized we had left my little niece Lisette locked in the car. I said (to my mother),

"Give me the car keys," but she was very lethargic so I screamed at her, hysterical—
"Give me the keys, Lisette is locked in the car, and if she wakes up like that she'll
be really scared—give me the keys." She did and I started running down hallways,
stairs, through a lobby, through lots of people. I was really hurting inside that I had
left Lisette locked in the car.

After sharing this dream Lori saw clearly that her own mother had never
taught her to care for her Inner Child (represented by her little niece Lisette
in the dream). Fortunately, the dream shows Lori activating her Nurturing/
Protective Parent Within and taking action in the face of her mother's
indifference. I pointed out that this dream occurred after she had decided to
have psychological consultation with me. Her Inner Self was validating her
decision and pointing her in the direction of finding help in learning to
nurture the Child Within. Which brings us to the second dream in the
series:

Dream # 2: Facing Obstacles with Help

Then a woman (about my age) and I were trying to get up from somewhere with
a white dress bag. We were climbing a hill and I was wearing my black heels. We
were confronted with a sheer rock face with a silver-gray metal fence at the top. I
gave the dress bag to the woman. She went first and I went holding on to the fence
pole with my left hand, stepping along the granite and coming along the side. Then
there was a ladder which was shiny, encrusted metal that I was trying to go up. I
didn't like it so I looked for an alternate route.

In relating this dream, Lori saw that the woman who was helping her
represented the part of herself that was thoroughly capable of solving her
own problems and being neither a rescuer nor a victim. And in fact, it was
an internalized aspect of this woman helper who appears later as Lori
herself in the fourth dream.

Dream # 3: Comfort and Acceptance

Then I was with Richard (my ex-boyfriend) and Billy (a close personal friend). I
was trying to cuddle with Richard, but he was un-cooperative, so Billy kissed me
a peck on the lips. I was playful and puckered my lips like a fish—he kissed me
anyway and smiled. Then, he held me and it was very comforting.

This dream shows Lori's pattern of being in relationships with men who are emotionally unavailable to her (represented by former boyfriend Richard). It also shows the pattern of masking the hurt and abandoned Child Within through silliness, sarcasm, and play-acting. Although it was difficult for her to accept affection when it was offered, her antics did not push Billy away. He was still there for her in spite of her distancing behavior, showing her a kind of unconditional acceptance that left her feeling comforted.

Dream # 4: Standing Up to the Controlling Father

My father called me on the phone and said he wanted me to see a Dr. Duvall and to come home and rest and get well there and that he would see that I had what I needed. I told him I hadn't made up my mind yet what I was going to do, and that I would make my own decision and let him know what I had decided. I said, "Don't call me and bother me again about this," and I hung up.

In this last of the series of dreams that Lori had in one night, we come full circle back to the parent/child relationship. Lori realized that her father, a very wealthy and powerful man, had always tried to control and manipulate her. In doing so he had disempowered her and made her feel incapable of taking care of herself and leading a life of her own. In this dream Lori "grows up" and asserts herself as an independent individual who can make her own decisions and find the path to healing that is best for her. She becomes her own parent.

In some cases, the Spiritual Child may reveal itself directly in a dream. Such dreams usually usher in a spiritual renewal. Shortly after meeting the great meditation master Swami Muktananda, I was visited by such a dream. In the dream, I was bowing to Muktananda as he sat on his chair receiving visitors. Looking back up, I saw him dissolve, and in his place sat the adult-size image of myself as an infant. This is how I appeared in the first formal photographs taken of me when I was six months old. In that photo, I am a blissful infant, a baby Buddha. Looking at the picture has always brought a smile to my face and a feeling of warmth and love to my heart. In the dream, I heard Muktananda's voice saying, "Honor your Self. God exists in you as you." At the time I had this dream, I had been meditating and nurturing my spiritual needs in a deeper way than ever before. This dream marked a turning point in my spiritual life.

Photo of Lucia, six months old.

It is important to point out here that the age of the child in your dreams is significant. If you ask yourself what was happening in your life when you were that age, there is usually a strong connection to what is going on now. For instance, when I was six months old I was baptized. That could be interpreted as my first spiritual initiation. About six months prior to my dream of Muktananda, I had begun meditating and experiencing the God Within. A new Spiritual Child was born at that time. At the time of the dream it was six months old and was being initiated (baptized) again.

This correlation between the Inner Child's age, what happened when you were that age, and what is going on now also applies to drawings and dialogues. For instance, when I first experienced my Inner Child in therapy,

I felt about four and a half years old. At the time I began therapy I was suffering from a collagen disease. Four and a half years earlier, my marriage and business partnership and my parents' marriage had begun to disintegrate. It was a time of "falling apart."

When I was four and a half, my parents moved away from the Italian neighborhood where they had been raised and where I had been cared for by a grandmother, aunts and uncles, and cousins. I felt uprooted and disconnected from family. Those were the same feelings I had during my divorce.

THE CHILD IN YOUR DREAMS

MATERIALS: Paper and felt pens.

1. If a child appears spontaneously in your dreams, you can discover its message by drawing a picture of it with your non-dominant hand. Then write an interview. With your dominant hand ask the child in your dream what it has come to show you. The child answers with your non-dominant hand. Then ask the child in your dream what it wants from you. Close your interview by thanking the child for appearing and delivering its message.

2. If you would like to receive messages from your Inner Self or Higher Power, write a letter before you go to sleep. Ask for a dream to show you how to best re-parent your Inner Child. If there is something troubling you in everyday life, ask for guidance about that particular issue. Thank your Inner Self or Higher Power for responding to your request for guidance.

Dear Inner Self,

Please give me a dream tonight that will tell me how to take better care of my own Inner Child.

Love,

Maria had this powerful and transformational dream in which her Inner Child appeared, heralding a deep healing process.

I was asleep in my bed. I saw myself get out of bed. I leaned against my dresser. My body remained in bed looking like a deflated balloon.

There was an invisible child inside the empty body. I could sense her presence but only saw her little fingers hanging on to the empty eye sockets. Together we watched a vision at the head of the bed. It was like a dream within a dream. I saw myself, as an adult, handing a yellow daisy to a child (myself) about five years old. I said to her, "Everything is going to be all right, Gloria." Though I couldn't see the child in the adult body, I could sense her joy.

I then got back into bed and into my body. All the other selves disappeared and I slept soundly until morning.

Your Spiritual Child of the Past

The more re-parenting work I have done, the more deeply I have felt the presence of my divine Spiritual Child. It is clear that she was always there, even in early childhood. At age seven (on the eve of my First Holy Communion) I had a profound dream about spiritual awakening. In the dream I was sitting alone in the front pew of our parish church. I glanced to the right of the main altar and noticed that the statue of St. Joseph holding the Infant Jesus was coming to life. The next thing I knew it had become the adult Christ, but he was made of light. This Christ figure came toward me, sat next to me on my right, and held my hand. We sat quietly together and he sent love to me silently. When I awoke I felt deeply at peace. I also remembered the texture of Christ's hand holding mine, as if it had been a tangible physical experience. I never shared this dream with anyone, because I was afraid they would ridicule me or accuse me of lying. Even at age seven, I knew the dream was real and far too precious to expose to the ignorance of others. So I kept it in my heart as a sign of God's love for me.

Around the same age, I began meditating spontaneously. I did not know what meditation was, so I never had a name for it. What happened was that a phrase would repeat itself in my mind, like a mantra: "Lucia, you are your Self, you are your Self, you are your Self." It was clear that this Self was different from my everyday personality self. Being a child, I did not have the intellectual and verbal skills to articulate the experience. But if I were alone and quiet, it was very easy for me to hear the words repeating in my mind. I would drift out into the universe and feel that I was flying among the stars and the galaxies. I became one with all creation. The feeling was one of deep peace and serenity. Again, I never told anyone about these experiences, because I did not know how. Even if I could have talked about it, I did not want to risk being misunderstood or laughed at. This was a cherished and mysterious secret between me and God. Many years later, when I was introduced to meditation by Swami Muktananda, I finally understood that what I had been doing in those early years was meditating. My Spiritual Child Within had entered meditation as naturally as breathing, effortlessly and without fear.

You may have had some spiritual experiences in childhood that were very personal and private. They may have happened in any number of ways. You may even have forgotten all about them. Or you may have later dismissed them as childish or strange. The next exercise will give you an opportunity to revive any such experiences from your early years and to appreciate them for what they really were: the expressions of your Spiritual Child.

SPIRITUAL CHILD OF THE PAST

MATERIALS: Paper and felt pens.

1. With your non-dominant hand, let your Spiritual Child of the Past write about any spiritual experiences from your childhood. These may have been dreams, visions, meditations, or special events that were charged with spiritual meaning.

2. Ask your Spiritual Child to draw a picture of itself in one of these experiences.

i wanted to be a
hermit and live in a
cave and be friends
with the animals like
St francis of assisi.
i wanted peace &
order & harmony.
i talked & sang to God
a lot. i played music
on the piano from my heart.

when i played i made
up music
and i knew it was
beautiful and i
was happy
it felt like God was
smiling when i
played.

Meeting Your Spiritual Child

The following is a guided meditation to meet your Spiritual Child. It is preferable to do this with your eyes closed, so you may want to read the text into a tape recorder and then play it back. Whether you tape it or remember it, it is best to get into a relaxed state. You can either sit or lie down comfortably with your eyes closed.

Imagine that you are walking down a little dirt path in a woods. It is a beautiful spring day. Everything is new green. The ground is covered with wildflowers—purple, pink, yellow, and white. Everything smells fragrant and fresh. Birds are warbling overhead and the sunlight is pouring down through the leaves. You feel very safe here surrounded by nature, by beauty, by the flowers, trees, birds, and sunlight.

As you walk down the path you suddenly come to a little clearing. And in the middle of this clearing is a little chapellike building. It is very small, with a pitched roof and a plain wooden door. You can feel that there is something very magical about this place. As you approach, the door opens and a little child comes out onto the front step. The child smiles at you and invites you to come in. As you get nearer and look more closely into this child's face you realize that it is you—it is your own Spiritual Child. The Child welcomes you and tells you it has been waiting for you and is so glad to see you.

Then your Spiritual Child asks you to take off your shoes and come in. The Child takes your hand and leads you in. You find yourself in a small carpeted room, filled with the scent of cedar wood. There is no furniture, only two pillows on the floor. The room is illuminated by a soft light coming from the opposite wall. You notice that it is actually sunlight coming through a circular pattern of dots cut out of the wooden wall. The Child motions you to sit on one of the pillows on the floor facing the circle of light. The Child sits next to you on the other pillow. Together, you quietly contemplate the circle of light. You feel the holiness of this place. As you sit, a beautiful feeling of peace and love envelops you. You feel as if you have come home to yourself.

After a while, the Child invites you to come outside into the sunlight.

You go out and sit together on a little wooden bench under the green trees. And there, you talk to your Spiritual Child. You find that although this little Child is very young, it seems to have great wisdom. It speaks with simplicity and clarity from the heart. It knows you well. When you are through talking, you embrace your Spiritual Child and invite it home to live in your heart.

A HEART-TO-HEART TALK

MATERIALS: Paper and felt pens.

1. Write out a dialogue with your Spiritual Child. With your dominant hand ask any questions you would like. Let the Spiritual Child respond with your non-dominant hand.

2. Draw a picture of any aspect of the guided meditation in which you met your Spiritual Child.

3. Draw a picture of your Spiritual Child with your non-dominant hand.

The following series of dialogues with the Spiritual Child were done by participants at a weekend workshop on re-parenting.

DIALOGUE WITH SPIRITUAL CHILD

Adult: You know me best—what can you tell me?

Child: You are on the right path. Take your time to stay in touch. You need to focus & avoid distractions like too much T.V. Listen to me—meditate, take care of your body which is your temple so that you can have creative energy. Take time to visualize. Remember to be grateful.

DIALOGUE WITH SPIRITUAL CHILD

Adult: I want to ask you Spiritual Child to help me contact my Higher Power.

Child: You want to. Do it. I am here with you. All you have to do is ask & I am always there. I am your best self. I am SELF & connection to all. I am all healing. I am within you & between you & others. Don't be afraid to be vulnerable. No one will hurt you. Reach out to others. You are contacting me & yourself. You are already there. Others want to be touched. I love you. You want to be touched. Trust me. Let yourself go to the ecstasy. There is pain there too, but I am holding & embracing you. You will not perish but return again. I enfold you. You are my champion. WE are one when you can touch others thru and in me. You are whole because you are as cells of the same body. Your/my consciousness is one. I love you. Love me. Love one another, Love. Love yourself!!! And you will love all.

DIALOGUE WITH SPIRITUAL CHILD

Adult: Am I to continue with my writing, Holy Friend? Is it part of the function you have designed for me?

Child: You have the answer inside—always look within where you will find me who is yur SELF. I am always with you you are never without yur SELF. That is why I would have u write 2 put yur reality down on paper so others will find / recognize their connectedness as yu have yours. Honor the process nurture it and you will draw 2 yur SELF like people. U experience what is real what is not—what has meaning what has not thru the art / function / process of writing. It is how I came 2 life 4 u. It is how I will remain a living active part of u here. U tried living without me to deny me and u almost died. Nurture me water me tend me. Put me on paper so u can share me an keep me.

SPIRITUAL CHILD DIALOGUE

Adult: What do I need to do to nurture my Inner Child?

Child: You need to structure some time for her. You need to clear some crap out of your life. You need to take better care of your physical body. You need to seek out fun people. You need to make art & music and play with Charlie. You need to fix-up your play space. Maybe get a new play space & spend time in the woods, build a (Kay drew a teepee here).

Risk doing things differently.
Spend time with kids.
Form a group
Write
Own me.

The Spiritual Child appears in many different forms in people's drawings. Sometimes it looks very ethereal, at other times it has the quality of primitive art. Occasionally the Spiritual Child is rendered in a portrait-style likeness. The next two drawings, one by Sue and another by Kate, show very different perceptions of the Spiritual Child. In Sue's drawing, the Child appears almost as a fairy princess. One can almost see star dust surrounding her, and her name is Urfin-Starchild.

Kate, who considers herself a non-artist, drew this picture of her Spiritual Child at a workshop. She had never attempted drawing people before, and was amazed at the results, especially because she did it with her non-dominant hand.

The ultimate "parent," the greatest teacher and healer, is our own spiritual guidance, in whatever form it appears. Some people hear a voice in their heart or see an image. For others, guidance comes through meditation or prayer or when they write out their innermost thoughts and feelings.

We all have different names and definitions for inner guidance, depending on our religious upbringing, cultural roots, or chosen spiritual path. It is essential that we acknowledge spiritual guidance as something that belongs to us. Like creativity, it is our natural birthright. We can call it whatever we wish: God, Holy Spirit, Higher Self, Universal Mind, Higher Power, or Inner Self. The important thing is to experience it in whatever form it expresses and to receive its healing power.

It is this Spiritual Guide Within who gives us the strength to re-parent our Inner Child. This is our unlimited source of love—making it possible for us to heal and be whole.

DIALOGUE WITH A SPIRITUAL GUIDE

MATERIALS: Paper and felt pens.

1. Imagine a person whom you regard as a spiritual guide or wise being who embodies the spirit of love, compassion, and dedication to principles of peace and justice. This is a person who *lives* these principles in his or her everyday life. It can be someone alive or someone who is no longer living. It can be someone from history or from the great traditions of spiritual masters. It is important that this person has meaning for you as a guide to your own inner strength and wisdom, especially as it relates to healing your Inner Child.

2. Have a dialogue with your Spiritual Guide. Ask questions with your dominant hand and let your Spiritual Guide respond with your non-dominant hand. Be sure to ask it for specific guidance in healing your Inner Child. How can it help you to do this? What do you need to know? What do you need to do to love and cherish your very own Inner Child? When you are through, thank your Spiritual Guide for its love and assistance in your healing process.

In a workshop at a spiritual retreat center, participants wrote dialogues. Although the guides had different names, they all sounded the same when group members read aloud. As one woman observed: "It is all one voice."

GUIDANCE FROM HIGHER POWER

Inner Parent: What shall I do next? What do I need to know to help this Inner Child?

Higher Power: Light candles! Make banners! Speak from the Heart! CELEBRATE!

GUIDANCE FROM THE SPIRITUAL SELF

Guide: Trust me. This is an evolution. Allow yourself to be with your feelings. This is the key. Allow yourself to cry. Don't be so strong. Let the child experience all the feelings not just the good ones. Spend more time alone to work on your own process & be with the child. Stop filling every day and night with activities. Read more and write more. Introspection. Get to know the kid and ask it what it wants often. Pray for guidance. Once you get to know it let it lead you in many areas of your life. Don't be so concerned with playing. Make time to be alone with your thoughtful child. The one who felt so close to God, so close to nature, so close to animals.

DIALOGUE WITH HIGHER POWER

Adult: Give me the guidance that I need right now in my life, Higher Power:

Higher Power: Use what I have given you. You are the gift. You are perfect. You need not look outside yourself for light, for peace; for answers. I am inside you. All you have to do is remember. I am you and you are light you are peace. You have the answers. But you are not on this journey alone. You must share what's inside you with others. You cannot learn alone. There are no accidents. We are all here for the same reason which is to love. Do what you love for that is why I made you. I am love. Discover what I am not and you will have found your life.

DIALOGUE WITH HIGHER POWER

Adult: Higher Power—Holy Spirit, Great spirit, talk to me. Be with me.

Higher Power: My Dear Child, I am always with you just like your breath and your beating heart I sustain you to be come aware stop a second and pay attention. You, Hear Me. I am so happy you brought your precious with you. Doesn't it feel good to hold her while you sit with me? I embrace the 2 of you. I envelop you with my Peace and Love and Protection. What do you want to ask me?

Adult: I've learned much this weekend. And I want to go home & be loving and peaceful but I'm afraid they'll be crying, complaining or arguing & I'll buy into it & get hooked & my regular ole self will come back & all this growth this weekend won't be enough to deal with the home stuff. Will you help me?

Higher Power: . . . . You can be your old self & be crabby & slip & get hooked. I will unhook you. I will gently draw a smile on your face. I will remind you to close your eyes & take a second to remember Me & My Love for my children remember my children left my home put on their body suits to live & be with you just like you did to be with them. I am always with you. I am always with them. Talk to me inside of them. Ask for me that way. I am the light. I am the peace. I am the Beauty I am Love I am me I am you I am the Great Spirit

Adult: Amen

I would like to leave you with this beautiful letter written by Kate to her Inner Child. It describes a healthy cherished Inner Child as seen through the eyes of a loving Inner Parent. May you be blessed, as she was, to find and love that pure essence and divine joy, the Inner Child that lives in your heart.

Beloved Child—

How blessed I am at your presence in my life—how joyous to feel laughter bubbling up from such a deep and wondrous space.

I value so much getting lost in time with you—of becoming and experiencing my creativity through you—& my increased awareness and intuitive functioning. I love the innocence.

The pure essence, divine joy that is so much you—the acceptance of all things and beings without judgment—but discernment—you are the smile in my eyes, the unconditional love in my heart, the trust and optimism that I feel. You are who I get lost in the moment with hopping boulders in wild canyons—the one pained at the cruelty of humans and other beings. You are the wonder in my life—the freedom from strangling responsibility. Unbridled creativity dancing in my being—I love you. Stay and play with me.

The child and the wise old man were balanced in him. His eyes were still bright as a bird's.

—Peggy Pond Church
The House at Otowi Bridge

Bibliography

ABRAMS, JEREMIAH. Edited by *Reclaiming the Inner Child.* Los Angeles, Jeremy P. Tarchler, 1990.

BARDSLEY, SANDRA AND LUCIA CAPACCHIONE. "The Creative Birth Journal: A Tool for Accessing the Right Side of the Brain." *Genesis,* Vol. 10, No. 5, June/July 1988, pp. 9–11.

BEATTIE, MELODY. *Beyond Codependency.* San Francisco, Harper & Row, 1989.

———. *Codependent No More.* New York, Harper/Hazelden, 1987.

BLACK, CLAUDIA. *It Will Never Happen to Me.* Colorado, Medical Administration, 1980.

BLOOMFIELD, HAROLD H., with LEONARD FELDER. *Making Peace with Your Parents.* New York, Ballantine Books, 1983.

BRADSHAW, JOHN. *Homecoming.* New York, Bantam, 1990.

CAMPBELL, JOSEPH, with BILL MOYERS. *The Power of Myth*. New York, Doubleday, 1988.

CAPACCHIONE, LUCIA. *The Power of Your Other Hand*. N. Hollywood, Newcastle, 1988.

————. *The Creative Journal*. N. Hollywood, Newcastle, 1989.

————. *The Well-Being Journal*. N. Hollywood, Newcastle, 1989.

————. *The Creative Journal for Children*. Boston, Shambhala Publications, 1989.

————. *The Picture of Health*. Santa Monica, Hay House, 1990.

CAPPACCHIONE, L., E. JOHNSON, and J. STROHECKER. *Lighten Up Your Body, Lighten Up Your Life*. N. Hollywood, Newcastle, 1990.

DAVIS, BRUCE. *The Magical Child Within You*. Berkeley, Celestial Arts, 1985.

HAY, LOUISE L. *You Can Heal Your Life*. Santa Monica, Hay House, 1987.

————. *Heal Your Body*. Santa Monica, Hay House, 1982.

————. *I Love My Body*. Santa Monica, Hay House, 1987.

————. *The AIDS Book: Creating a Positive Approach*. Santa Monica, Hay House, 1988.

————. *Forgiveness/Loving the Inner Child* (audiotape). Santa Monica, Hay House, 1989.

JUNG, C. G. and C. KERENYI. *Essays on the Science of Mythology: The Myth of the Divine Child*. Princeton, Bollingen Series, 1969.

KASL, CHARLOTTE DAVIS. *Women, Sex and Addiction*. New York, Ticknor & Fields, 1989.

KRITSBERG, WAYNE. *The Adult Children of Alcoholics Syndrome*. Pompano Beach, FL, Health Communications, 1986.

MELLODY, PIA, with MILLER, A., and MILLER, J. *Facing Codependence*. San Francisco, Harper & Row, 1989.

MILLER, ALICE. *For Your Own Good: Hidden Cruelty in Child-Rearing and the Roots of Violence.* New York, Farrar, Straus & Giroux, 1984.

———. *Thou Shalt Not Be Aware: Society's Betrayal of the Child.* New York, Farrar, Straus & Giroux, 1984.

———. *Pictures of a Childhood.* New York, Farrar, Straus & Giroux, 1988.

MISSILDINE, W. HUGH. *Your Inner Child of the Past.* New York, Simon & Schuster, 1963, and Pocket Books, 1982.

MUKTANANDA, SWAMI. *Meditate.* South Fallsburg, NY, SYDA Foundation, 1980.

PEARCE, JOSEPH CHILTON. *Magical Child: Rediscovering Nature's Plan for Our Children.* New York, Bantam Books, 1986.

POLLARD, JOHN H. *Self Parenting: The Complete Guide to Your Inner Conversations.* Malibu, CA, Generic Human Studies, 1987.

SCHAEF, ANN WILSON. *Co-Dependence: Misunderstood-Mistreated.* San Francisco, Harper & Row, 1986.

SENDAK, MAURICE. *Where the Wild Things Are.* New York, Harper & Row, 1964.

STONE, CHRISTOPHER. *Re-Creating Your Self.* Portland, Metamorphous Press, 1988.

STONE, HAL and SIDRA WINKELMAN. *Embracing Our Selves.* San Rafael, New World Library, 1989.

———. *Embracing Each Other.* San Rafael, New World Library, 1989.

WHITFIELD, CHARLES L. *Healing the Child Within.* Deerfield, FL. Health Communications, 1987.

———. *A Gift to Myself.* Health Communications, 1990.

———. *Synopsis of Co-dependence.* Health Communications, 1991.

———. *Boundaries, Relationships, and Recovery.* Health Communications, (book in process).

WILLIAMS, MARGERY. *The Velveteen Rabbit.* Garden City, Doubleday & Co., 1969.